Guiding Children's Reading through Experiences

Guiding Children's Reading through Experiences

Second Edition

ROMA GANS
Professor Emeritus
Teachers College, Columbia University

Teachers College, Columbia University
New York and London 1979

Library of Congress Cataloging in Publication Data

Gans, Roma, 1894-
  Guiding children's reading through experiences.

  Bibliography: p.
  Includes index.
  1. Reading (Elementary) I. Title.
LB1573.G25 1979   372.4′1   79-16407
ISBN 0-8077-2569-2

Designed by Romeo M. Enriquez
9 8 7 6 5 4 3 2 1   86 85 84 83 82 81 80 79
Manufactured in the United States of America

Contents

PART II: READING IN THE ELEMENTARY SCHOOL

Foreword

Roma Gans is the Will Rogers of education! Her ideas, child-centered for the most part, are down-to-earth, practical, creative, and effective. She presents them with wit and wisdom honed on eighty plus years of genuine living. Not only does she accept each student's individuality, but she also delights in the challenges presented in each child's uniqueness.

Therefore, it is not surprising to find this revised edition of *Guiding Children's Reading through Experiences* to be a professional gem. Roma speaks out loudly and clearly about teachers, children, parents, and a love of reading. She strikes hard at the hucksters and the so-called theorists who are trying to make teaching a pure science rather than what it really is—reaching impossible dreams (and really being successful in so many ways). In her view, teaching is an emotion-filled, surprising, romantic adventure.

To succeed in this venture, Roma shows the need to relate skills instruction to the actual context of reading materials in different subject areas. Children need to be motivated through the use of interesting materials and experiences, and they need time to apply and practice the skills that are essential for further reading, understanding, and enjoyment. This does not require gadgetry; busy workbook pages; excessive expenditures on packages, management systems, and kits; what is needed is a teacher who knows the students and who can plan the best programs to meet their different needs. Obviously, such a teacher should be flexible and resourceful. Roma offers many excellent ideas for developing the real professionals who love children, enjoy teaching, and are avid readers themselves.

This book recognizes that reading is a personal and active process. Each reader responds in his or her own way to the printed message. Developing and encouraging these responses are, indeed, essential steps for producing independent readers who will enjoy reading for the many purposes in their lifetimes.

Roma's references to such distinguished colleagues as Nancy Larrick, Jean Piaget, Herbert Kohl, Stuart Chase, and Frank Jennings, among many others, indicate her genuine concern that teachers recognize the many disciplines they need to acknowledge as possible approaches in the teaching of reading. The complex processes involved in learning how to read require constant study by all of those who are interested in how children develop intellectually, socially, emotionally, and physically. Studying a child's environments and experiences can reveal much about why he succeeded and another had difficulties.

This book is inspirational. Anecdotes and guidelines clearly emphasize that readers come from teachers who find that their work provides them with a good measure of personal satisfaction. Few teachers, if any, will walk away from this book without feeling better for having discovered it and the delightful woman whose ways with words encourage thinking and acting with confidence and compassion.

That's what Roma's all about!

M. JERRY WEISS

Jersey City State College

Perspective

IN 1917 WHEN I BEGAN TEACHING, I HAD MY FIRST CONTACT WITH reading in the lives of children other than those in my own family. All of us in the family, while growing up, read newspapers, the comics, magazines, current novels, and books of all kinds—some classics and some trash. Of course, we read assigned texts and "did our homework," some of it assigned reading.

But I was to receive a shock in my first years of teaching—upper grades and high school. The majority of youngsters read nothing except school-assigned reading: no newspapers, books, not even comics.

This raised a question in my mind that persists, "Why teach reading?" When I asked two amiable assignment achievers, "Don't you miss not reading anything outside of schoolwork?" one responded, "How can we miss it when we are out of school?"

Most of the oncoming waves of excitement over research discoveries, I confess, did not stir me. Eye movements—their speed and regressive movements—the edict to use flash cards, and an actual ban on oral reading in all grades did not stop me from reading news accounts and stories to pupils who always listened eagerly.

World War I, of course, was the big concern. Many of my students had close relatives overseas in combat. I would read the headlines; later the most eager read the entire accounts. Weather predictions and sports events were also of interest.

Since there were no school libraries in my hometown—St. Cloud, Minnesota—and limited children's books in the public library, my only reading resource was from my home. Many students became interested in *St. Nicholas* magazine, and a few borrowed my copy of *Silas Marner*.

Each Monday morning I faithfully carried the Sunday comic sections to my classroom; groups read them in small snatches of time. The students loved Andy Gump and the Katzenjammer Kids. This was a popular part of my bootleg reading program, when I was one of the teachers of algebra.

Following World War I in the twenties, the era of the IQ was launched. Education as a science was thus introduced. Standardized tests in reading (and other subjects), vocabulary lists, homogeneous grouping, and new promotion policies followed, as well as, of course, "scientifically controlled vocabulary" textbooks.

Not all were caught up in this surge. Early childhood life became the focus of research by noted child-development specialists. They studied the language and social development of young children and their thinking.

The real pulse of education began to throb in the 1920s. Through Freud's influence, deeper psychological concerns emerged that stimulated educators to study the emotional factors affecting children. And, thanks especially to John Dewey, who emphasized children's learning through experiences, which he explored at the Frances Parker School, a genuine awakening stirred the nation's educators. The progressive education movement began: experimentation in the schools in more unified, certainly less piecemeal, programs popped up across the country. Education became a live topic with adherents of the "scientific" approach opposing those of the "learning-by-experience" emphasis.

Children were not only taught to read and to read text, but also to use reading in their wider curriculum studies. The so-called "modern" schools, both public and private, in the middle twenties included libraries with books of all kinds to fit the burgeoning interests of groups and individuals. This was an exciting time in education. Teachers of that period found teaching truly challenging.

In all of my contacts with schools, there never has been a period when the climate was stagnant. Instead, there always has been a stream of the "latest ideas." This reached an all-time deluge with the advent of sputnik. Schools were suddenly discovered to be remiss, especially in the development of know-how in science and math. Curriculum studies became more prevalent than reducing diets. No doubt, this concern lead to the continuing "back-to-basics" wave.

Special interest in reading across the nation received a boost by two big events, the enactment of the federal Right-to-Read Program and the federally financed projects under Title I. Many teachers in the Right-to-Read Program received aid from the specific suggestions for developing a goal-centered program.

Millions of the Title I funds, however, were squandered on ideas that were quacky. Some, like the spurious phonic panaceas promoted after the *Why Johnny Can't Read* earth tremor, were spawned by the search for the real elixir— *a foolproof system of teaching every child to read.* Countless millions were spent on this one hunt.

Fortunately, many other forces over all these years plodded ahead, often with zeal but with little or no money. Teachers, who themselves were truly functional readers, guided those who came into their orbit to read with increased personal ability and satisfaction. Parents, individually and in groups, increased the youngsters' reading in everyday home life. And librarians, those too-often underpaid and neglected wards of literacy, spent almost superhuman efforts to bring the evergrowing number of fine, beautiful books of all kinds to readers—from preschoolers to adolescents.

Not to be overlooked or even given a lesser spot, however, was the fortunate trend that emphasized the individual. For eons, individual differences had been recognized and studied and written about. Yet uniformity, in methods, materials, and expected learnings, were continued. That line is now being broken. Special programs for the gifted are mandated in some states. And special classes and remedial programs, especially in reading, are now common.

Many of the remedial programs now proliferating at a terrific speed are the result of the genuine respect for each child's reading growth, no matter what his or her wherewithal. It is regrettable, though, that often the research, the methods, and materials in this field stress such vivisection of the reading process that not only to the child but to the intelligent teacher the efforts cannot be recognized as anything connected with reading. An antivivisectionist society is needed to protect especially the children, who are the victims, from this so-called remedial treatment.

In a recent visit to what was considered a "good reading" school, youngsters below the class norm were not allowed to read library books. They took their remedial reading work to the library on "library day" while others exchanged their library books. Why teach them to read?

The conscientious educator has been bombarded with "the latest thing in reading" so often that one may think the entire research and materials production field is filled with persons who have a genius in quackery. Not so.

In spite of these digressions, a sound concern for functional reading is moving ahead. After my sixty years of observations of children's reading, I still visit many classrooms where children are excited about books, authors, and illustrators; where teachers and parents are demanding more library resources. The emphasis on reading is not for "plain book larnin' " or to raise the test-score norms, but to develop readers who use reading to propel themselves in life much as they use their legs.

Does this mean my major concern about functional reading from the earliest years on has been met? Not yet. There are still many with hangovers of the so-called scientific era and still many others to whom becoming a reader through experiencing reading seems too pleasant a way to learn. The majority, though, who have a concern about the oncoming generations, continue to boost the cause of reading as an essential power in daily life. Included in this group are valiant teachers, parents, librarians, book publishers, and dedicated citizens. For them, I decided to rewrite *Guiding Children's Reading through Experiences*. This new edition makes its focus relevant to children in these times.

PART **1**

Reading Begins:
Preschool Years

CHAPTER **1**

Language—The First Step

LIKE TRIBAL MORES, IN WHICH AT A GIVEN AGE THE CHILD IS inducted into the skill of hunting, so our young children at about the age of six are inducted into reading. But unfortunately for many of the children of our land, learning to read is not as easy as learning to hunt; and many who meet with difficulty en route may do so because those who try to teach them do not understand how children take hold of this complicated skill.

Unlike learning to use a weapon in hunting, reading is not demonstrable. Therefore, it is not readily acquired by imitation or merely by watching those who read.

Children acquire much in the first years merely by living within their families and taking on their ways. They learn to speak their language, with the family's idioms and characteristics. They take a comb and try to comb their hair. They untie their shoes and try to tie them as they have seen others do. They use the telephone, turn on the tap for a drink of water, eat cereal, try to use a ball-point pen, and open a book to a page just as they have seen parents and siblings do.

Concern about failures in reading is expressed with increasing intensity as studies of upper grades and high school reveal. It actually explodes when college data are publicized. Such intellectually maimed students doubtlessly got their reading lacks in their preschool or early school experiences. For this reason, I stress the analysis and the important role of home and school in the early years in the development of competent functional readers.

UNDERSTANDING THE WAY THE YOUNG CHILD LEARNS

The actual process of reading, whether oral or silent, cannot be imitated. To a child, it must seem like a very mysterious business. Often a child will hand a book to his or her mother and say, "Read this." Then the child will look from the book to her face and back again at the book with a puzzled expression. And no wonder. Almost everything else she or he has asked her to do could be observed, maybe helped with, and later imitated. If children's difficulty with latching onto what one does while reading were adequately understood by parents, and by nursery-school and primary-grade teachers, they would receive real help in learning to read and would consequently learn with greater ease and with more promise of functional reading in future life.

WHEN TALKING BEGINS—THE CHILD'S METHOD

Would that all of us who teach children to read could observe the method of beginning to speak among infants. At first they start with a syllable or sound, "da" or "ma," then they actually struggle to master a word such as "doggie." We hear their first efforts, which are not exactly correct. We see the serious expression on their faces as they listen to the word pronounced for them. They try again and look for the adult reaction, almost as if asking how they are doing. They give themselves practice or "drill" until they are satisfied and proceed to the next word.

But learning to read is a very different process from learning to speak. Reading demands interpreting symbols—symbols unlike toys, gadgets, or household things a child can use and name. The following observation will show a few of the intervening steps between a child's experience and one word, a collection of four symbols arranged in proper sequence to represent *baby*. Two sixteen-month-old infants were put into the same yard to play. Each eyed the other intently. Then one walked unsteadily toward the other and explored, touching his face, feeling his hair, and putting a finger in his eye. He looked toward his father and smilingly said, "Baby." He had had previous experience with babies so the word baby had meaning for him. It meant a real creature with eyes, hair to feel, a face and a body to touch. When this infant heard the word baby, he could visualize a baby.

Several weeks later, he was observed scrutinizing the picture of an infant on the cover of a magazine on the floor beside him. He tried to pinch the picture. He tried to put his finger in the eye on the picture. He leaned down and licked the picture. He looked puzzled as his mother said, "That's a baby." The child smiled and said, "Baby!" but continued to try to get the feel of this baby. Finally, with a sigh, he swept his hands quickly over the picture and crawled away. Several days later he came upon the same picture and, although still poking at it and trying to feel it, he smiled and said, "Baby!" He had learned to recognize the picture of an object he had previously experienced by touching and poking.

Several years later, when this child looks into a book and the word baby occurs, he must be able to picture a live baby by looking at those four letters that have absolutely no resemblance to an infant. This demands a huge step in growth toward the knowledge of symbols required by learning to read.

There is another crucial side to this phase of learning. Earlier, when the infant struggled with the picture, the efforts were observable. The mother knew the child was puzzled, and gave the right help. Later, she could also notice the child's growth in looking at pictures and recognizing them as representing the real thing. But when a young child is puzzled by how an adult reads or how one can tell what the word is, that perplexity is not so observable.

This is a part of many children's dilemma: they face something we expect them to learn, but it is so vague they cannot even ask intelligent questions about it; meanwhile, the adult cannot observe or sense their reactions. How often the adult, trying to be helpful, may say, "See, that word is dog"; but to the child the whole business of visualizing the meaning of the word, in size, color, or relationship, makes no sense. And if the word has never been experienced—like *tractor* to a city child or *escalator* to a rural youngster, who has never even seen an escalator on TV—no wonder reading growth is slow!

EARLY EXPERIENCES AND LEARNING

The study of how young children think continues and helps those who aim to guide them as intelligently as possible. But the inner workings of the child's mind in taking the steps necessary to get from symbols to words to their meanings are not yet fully understood. More apparent, but still amazing, is how a child acquires a functional vocabulary through playing, eating, watching anything that moves, and listening all the while. All this learning takes place without a teacher, a workbook, or the latest "scientific method."

All of us recognize some keys to such ability of the young child. We often say, "They miss nothing." True. Infants less than a year old have a store of recognizable items, people, and actions. If they are well and alert, they are learning. When they become toddlers, their constant busyness can be exhausting for the parent or baby-sitter who merely watches their activity. They inspect everything within their reach; they touch, taste, bang, and take apart. They initiate. They create. No boredom. If the home environment is safe for them, we can say they engage in self-propelled learning—essential to their age. When these experiences include conversations with adults or siblings, their functional vocabulary grows.

Such learning while being busy continues under normal living conditions. A five-year-old, who spent every Thursday with his father at his office, found "work" to do by himself. He separated the two sizes of paper clips and put them in two boxes. He collected the sealed envelopes from several desks and put them in the postbasket. He emptied the catchbasin at the water cooler when it became full. His vocabulary included *paper clips, water cooler, sealed envelope*—none familiar to his friends whose experiences were different. A four-year-old, Angela, helped her mother in the garden. She reported that she helped stake the tomatoes, thin the onions, and pick the snap beans. One can visualize these two youngsters being busy, doing something that they recognized as essential, and they were also acquiring the language that described what they did.

In contrast, young Jerry, when asked, "What did you do today in kindergarten that was important?" responded, "Cleanup time." Perhaps he did help mix paints and set his place for lunch. Often such chores are done with a minimum of conversation. The child fails to grow in the words to describe his or her actions.

No doubt in each group, there are the agile youngsters who hear a direction once and from then on remember it. But there are others who need to hear it repeated again and again. The lack of repetition is one reason for not learning on the part of the less nimble learners. If the kindergarten is a tightly prescribed program initiated by the teacher, with no opportunity for children's ideas, boredom is noticeable— especially for those of normal or above normal alertness. The contrast from a creative home life to a boring kindergarten can be stifling, even traumatic.

A kindergarten program with a variety of experiences going on, some continuing for days, with children talking over plans, making suggestions, trying out some of their own ideas, challenges the interests of the go-getters and often those not so overtly eager.

READINESS FOR FUTURE EXPERIENCES

Too often in pamphlets and books for parents, the importance of beginning language, though mentioned, is not stressed sufficiently. The early, proper growth in speech carefully observed by some parents, often neglected after the first word by others, has great importance to children's future life. Its effect on their intellectual maturing is a recognized fact. They seem wide-eyed, taking in everything that goes on around them. All senses are working full speed during their waking hours. And how they remember. They seem to have a mental glue that makes everything they hear stick.

Many youngsters, indeed fortunate ones, though born into an impoverished environment, have the good fortune to be spoken to, visited with, and treated as co-workers. Their language may reflect many sordid conditions others do not meet, but linguistically and intellectually they are growing.

We have no "loquacity quotient" for parents. Some may be ramblers, talk a lot, but say little. Often, adults politely tend to be listening, but aren't. Early in life children, too, learn to "turn it off"—often not politely. Other parents are mummers, say little, use one word directions to a child, with little repetition. Other parents, usually the sociable ones who enjoy life of all ages about them, use language keyed to the situation and the listener, child or adult. A child in the care of such an adult reaps the benefit. For the children under nonconversational care, today's media are a genuine blessing.

INFLUENCE OF THE MEDIA

The radio, which came upon the scene in most homes in the 1920s, began to erase what once could be called "the hinterland." Interest in current affairs spread from the city to the rural areas nationwide. And, of course, new interests and vocabulary grew to fit the topics. Families developed a communality through listening to programs, a wholesome factor.

Then came TV. With this new media, children of all ages acquired vicarious experiences far beyond those of previous years. With the viewing and listening came an extended awareness and in some ways a sophisticating influence. The shy, naive child, though not entirely extinct, is today almost a rarity. Instead of the creative, time-consuming plays and games of my childhood, youngsters today—from toddlers on—watch TV programs hour upon hour. A result, not often enough realized, was pointed out in a spicy way by a veteran teacher. "Thank God I'm about to retire! I get exhausted trying to teach with the pep and zing the kids expect today. I can't compete with television."

SIBLING AND NURSERY SCHOOL FACTORS

Another fact not often recognized is the influence of siblings on children's learning. The older ones serve as stimulators and models for the younger ones—an asset the only child misses until or unless he or she plays with peers at the age of about two.

Fortunately, nursery schools and day-care centers are growing in both urban areas and small communities. For the only child with too infrequent contacts with his or her peers, a nursery school should be considered a must.

CHAPTER 2

The Wonderful World of Symbols

I SHALL NEVER FORGET THE SURPRISE A YOUNG NEPHEW, AGED FOUR, gave me as we were standing on the railroad platform on 125th Street in New York City, waiting for a train. "What does that sign say?" he asked. There, on an old building, was the sign *Hirsute*. Although I had stood facing that sign many times, I actually never saw it before. Nor did I know then what it meant (hair—it was a place for wigs and hair pieces). Taking preschoolers on a shopping trip gives one many such surprises. Children are eagle-eyed; they notice signs, small items on buildings, odd mail slots that we have passed many times but have not noticed.

They recognize words that have meaning to them, like pizza, ice cream, and shakes. This is functional reading when they read the sign, often hoping for a treat. A supermarket is full of such reading opportunities for them.

READING—NOT READING READINESS

To me, the term *reading readiness* has always been a misnomer. When a preschooler looks at a sign and says, "Pizza," he or she is interpreting the symbols and is reading a word. Youngsters, if given proper adult attention, go through an exciting period of identifying signs, letters, insignia on automobiles, and labels on packages. Why should such evidence of learning be called reading readiness? This is real reading.

Such word recognition often is self-initiated. This is common to many alert three-year-old children. Not many years ago, teachers and parents were cautioned against early use of reading for fear of impairing their vision. Some cautioners even went so far as to say that the child's eyes "were not ready" for anything as small as letters. Phooey! Any baby-sitter can tell such alarmists that toddlers can spot some wee thing like a bead on a rug as they dash along. And how many parents have marveled at the eye-hand coordination of an infant eating the cookie crumbs off the plate. True, young children, even those who have considerable growth in reading, are not ready for the *formal minutely directed exercises* still used in all too many kindergartens as "reading readiness exercises," but their lack of readiness is not due to their vision or intellectual immaturity.

THE ABC'S

One of the first learning-to-read experiences I recall was singing the ABC's as my teacher pointed to each letter while we sang. I had learned the song from my older brother and we frequently sang it while playing at home. Of course, we had ABC blocks and played with them. We traced the letters with crayons, we copied them on scratch paper, and we wrote them in sequence. Later, as a teacher, I got the surprising advice that children were not to sing the ABC's nor learn to chant them in sequence. This was all a part of *rote memory*, which was verboten.

Recently, I heard a parent inquire over a question-answer program on the radio, "How dangerous is it for my four-year-old to learn the ABC's? He's interested in saying them and wants to write them too." The answer was, "This, if he is interested, can be joyful learning! Be glad that he wants to." So this fear based on a quacky idea still persists.

Part of this opposition to the early use of the ABC's came from discovering youngsters later on in the use of the dictionary who didn't know the sequence of the letters. This is no serious matter. They, themselves, can improvise games to satisfy this need. I have enjoyed watching a contest conducted by fourth graders in which speed in locating a word in the dictionary was the goal. The teacher reported that this contest originated when it was discovered that some were not sure of whether P followed Q or preceded it.

It is usually the bright fours and fives who want to know their ABC's, and also who want to be able to write them. To deny them is to frustrate them. They are ready to explore. If the writing becomes too difficult for them, they abandon it. A wise parent helps when it seems to add to the child's satisfaction and competence but does not press the child past his or her eagerness to continue.

BOOKS—BEGINNING OF A PERSONAL LIBRARY

"Sally is a hyperactive child, but when I hold her on my lap and read a story to her, she relaxes and often falls asleep," reported a mother at a meeting of a nursery school parent group. "Won't this dull her interest in stories?" asked another parent. "No. She now picks the book she wants me to read and often laughs as she relates humorous incidents. And, she guards her collection of books! Just try to move them from where she keeps them!"

Ownership of books with a genuine possessive feeling starts early—and continues. One father, who entered his child in kindergarten, said, "He's brought a few of his books. He wanted to take his whole library but I told him I didn't have a truck."

The growing increase in numbers of books produced for the before-they-read group is proof of the increased demand. And for a real thrill in book browsing, examine a few of the ABC books for young children. Those who still assume that the introduction is "A is for apple" will find themselves paging our latest ABC books with fascination. Recently, a mother brought her fourth grader with her to my home to inquire about some civic matter. The boy, Jerry, picked up *Albert B. Cub & Zebra,** an ABC book on the table. He was immediately intrigued and later said to his mother, "You ought to look at this book for young kids. It's great." She glanced hastily, then said, "Even I want to go through this from A to Z."

Book ownership helps develop proper care of books. Even in crowded homes, a carton bookcase can serve as the safe space for

*Anne Rockwell, *Albert B. Cub & Zebra: An Alphabet Storybook* (New York: Thomas Y. Crowell, 1977).

books. After browsing, a child can be reminded to put the book back in its safe home—and away from any toddlers who are still at the stage of tearing or tasting books.

Each added book can be an important event. A child may make an unsolicited comment like, "This is a good book," "Oh, what pretty pictures!" or "Why did you buy me this book? It's not any good." Young Candice liked "only animal books," her twin brother wanted "books with cars." Fortunately, whatever the current taste, books are available to sate it. But, it must also be added, more book stores and book departments in stores are needed, not only with an adequate supply but also with willingness to order wanted books. This critical need is extant, not only in smaller communities.

Children who are read to from early years can acquire not only the satisfaction of the personal attention but in addition some lasting effects that will boost their reading interests and know-how. The more they help by turning the page or filling in a word of a familiar story, the more reading means to them.

EARLY DEVELOPMENT OF TASTE

After handing a book to a woman lender with the comment, "This is one of the latest," a librarian recently said to me:

Too bad some adults didn't get the reading help today's kids get. This woman will read anything—if it's the latest. No preference—no taste. Youngsters come in, "Do you have more books about giraffes?" or "I want a story about real boys and girls." They are already selective and give pungent comments often as they return books. "Have you any more books by this author?" or "Kid stuff. I'm too old for this book."

The development of taste starts early; like any growing element, it needs encouragement. Young Danny, aged four, had just listened to a story read to him from a book given to him by his grandmother. After the reading, he asked, "Do I have to like this story because Grandy gave it to me?" "No," responded his father. "You thanked her for the book but you now tasted the story and you can like it or not like it." Had he said, "Oh, when Grandy gives you a book you've got to like it," he would have been searing a budding taster.

The Mark Twain Library in my home community had a peppy

reading program this summer for children—all ages. To test out their preferences, one point was the reading of a variety of books from fairy tales to biography. One ten-year-old said, "I read and enjoyed a lot, but I came back to my favorite—stories with some scary parts."

Part of this development of taste, of course, demands contacts with a wide collection of books. But, it also requires the encouragement of the readers to be honest with their reactions. They then develop the strength to stand up and be counted, as did eight-year-old Dwight, whom I taught in the third grade. One day, he held up a book that all of the others in the class said they liked. He fairly shouted, "I don't care if the whole world likes this book, I don't like it!"

THE BEGINNING SCRIBE

It is natural for children whose early learning is stimulated by imitation to move from scribbling to a desire to write. Certain letters in books or on TV may appeal to them. They may ask, "Show me how to make a *D*." The proper response is to write the letter so they can watch. Select a simple form, then describe writing, "First I make a straight line from the top down. Then I put a hoop on that line"—the description helps the child acquire the sequence. In these first uses of pencil or crayon, a child often reveals his handedness, if not before. Today, left-handedness is accepted; and, if accepted, the child suffers no handicap in any of his future activities.

Often, there is a great eagerness to write and much attention and help is demanded. Then, there may be a complete drop of interest. This waxing and waning of new ventures is normal behavior. Of course, there may be some loss by forgetting, but there also is a speedier pickup once the interest again takes hold.

FUNCTIONAL READING FROM EARLY EXPERIENCES

Preschoolers prove the old truism—they live and learn. They *will* to learn, to take hold, to manage. The dynamics of growth are evident. All they seem to need is exposure. They are unafraid to try themselves out, to imitate—and yes, to drill themselves. Repetition is self-applied, as needed. Many become readers before entering kindergarten and the majority, if healthy and not too restricted, have acquired an acquaintance with books, a mass of reading elements, like letters, some words, and awareness of the use of reading—to look up a telephone number, a recipe, or address, and to read the newspapers, mail, and advertisements.

So rapid is their growth that vocabulary studies become obsolescent before they can be completed. TV, radio, and travel have had tremendous impact on the before-five age group. From firsthand and vicarious experiences, they seem brighter, more mature, and more inquisitive than children of earlier years. The planning of programs appropriate for them, obviously must reflect this difference.

All who are so excited about the poor reading of high school graduates should give full support to programs of Head Start, nursery school, and family life. Here is where sound foundations are acquired. Not all youngsters will meet the expectations of critics. For some, the use of language and symbols is never a big accomplishment. We often refer to them as the nonverbal members of our community. They are worthy workers but not in the mental tricks communication demands. Some, however, with proper early experiences, also grow even beyond predictions. This is why informed educators and community leaders consider programs for the early years a priority. Longitudinal studies of the effect of preschool programs and family guidance in reading should reveal the actual saving of remedial work in junior and senior high schools and a decline in the number of pupils who fail.

FUN WITH PHONICS FOR PRESCHOOLERS

Preschool children also can enjoy the beginning of phonics. Children's play reveals their fascination with and use of sounds. The "z-z-z" while pushing along a miniature automobile, the chant of "bang, bang" while pounding one block upon another in building, and often just the "beep-beeping" as they run along indicates their enjoyment of sounds. Often, in the oral reading of an ABC book to them, the adult can stimulate and sharpen this interest in sounds. B can be exploded and other B words added. E can show front teeth with a broad smile, S "sizzles," and Z "zooms." Such pleasant experiences help the child to associate the sound with the letter—which is the beginning of phonics. Some youngsters go quickly from that to sounding out words that have some special appeal.

From experiences with the variety of sounds about them, children develop their hearing acuity. Their lack in developing this sharpness of hearing should rouse parents to have their children's hearing checked, although signs of a hearing problem are discovered earlier than four and five in today's health-care programs.

There has been such a to-do about phonics that many parents, yes, and nursery school teachers have developed a hands-off policy lest they do the wrong thing. Nonsense! Phonics is the association of sound and symbol. Any fun in this discovery and happy use is a good learning experience.

PART 2

Reading in the Elementary School

CHAPTER 3

A Veteran Teacher Takes a Critical Look

THE SCORES ON THE SCHOLASTIC APTITUDE TEST AND OTHER TEST scores revealing poor ratings in basic skills of high school seniors and college freshmen are being felt in the elementary school by what geologists call "the pressure of the overlying layers." The concern, both pro and con, deserves attention. The International Reading Association held many lengthy discussions on the popular urge to produce minimum competency standards.

The three divergent papers published in a pamphlet presented important points for all who are concerned. Kenneth Goodman discussed some common errors in attempting to meet the problem, especially through legislatively mandated minimum competencies; Robert Farr deplored the reliance on reading tests, suggesting "a variety of assessments, gathered at many points in a student's life"; Jack Cassidy, among a number of suggestions, included multilevel competencies, developed for primary grades, intermediate grades, and high school.*

To meet the reading needs of high school and college students is essential. A total program of improvement, however, demands a far more inclusive examination of the elementary school than has been conducted to date. By the time pupils get to later grades and college, some of their problems are not only deep but complex, sealed up, often with serious emotional kinks and even feisty attitudes. All too often the

---

*Jack Cassidy, Roger Farr, Kenneth Goodman, *Minimum Competency Standards: Three Points of View* (Newark, Del.: International Reading Association, 1978).

origins can be traced to the primary grades. The early school experience is the proper place to start a real inquiry, and many schools have already made strides in this.

Some of my observations indicate the depth and pervasiveness of the simple responsibility to teach them all to read successfully. The curriculum in today's school is crowded. To give each child adequate time for personal aid demands careful organization of minutes and tremendous know-how on the part of the teacher.

WHAT PROMOTES AND WHAT LIMITS SUCCESS IN READING?

Few critics are able to offer suggestions for improving reading, but most have a personal diagnosis, most commonly but vaguely: the schools. Those who can still feel when their skin is pricked, rightly deplore today's tempo and compulsive behavior, the growing flabbiness of the family fabric, the make-a-fast-buck predominance in our value scale, and even the influence of busing—the sapping of the young riders' interests and vitality. All are detracting influences. I have found from my own teaching and continued contacts with schools, however, there are three factors that fail to be mentioned.

School Attendance

The first of these three is frequent school absences. Returning to school, even after a brief absence, even for older youngsters, is an emotional shock. There is a feeling of not being with it, a loss—a hesitancy to take hold. For young children, even a one-day absence may have traumatic results. Only recently, an intelligent mother reported that her five-year-old Greta was sure her bus was not the right bus. Of course there are many with real power to adjust who take absences in stride and quickly feel at home, once back to school. These are often the nimble learners. But, the slower are often the ones who lose zip, and some seem never to recapture their learning pace.

In more recent times, caution over health needs has increased legitimate school absence. A child with a cold is kept home, not only to help him recover, but to protect his classmates.

Many communities have had long interruptions of daily work, however, due to strikes of teachers, parents, and community groups. The real damage to children's learning has never been properly assessed, but anyone close to such events can relate their toll, especially on the skills.

Daily attendance is taken all too lightly—even by the more conscientious parents who may keep youngsters from school for family trips, or baby-sitting responsibilities—then lie when presenting the excuse. How such a lax attitude affects youngsters' respect for the importance of their education cannot be precisely stated, but the all-too-common point of view, even among primary children, of "so what" or "who cares" is reflected in how casually they apply themselves to school-work.

Silence—Not Golden

Secondly, when research, years past, extolled the effects of silent reading to the exclusion of oral reading, the everyday educator swallowed a perpetuating pill! From then on—and to this day—oral reading by children has carried a negative coloring. Yet students, especially young children, have demonstrated their multisensory learning to observers from Montessori on: children see, they hear, they touch. Not only is speech important to the young child, as I discussed in chapter 1, but for beginning readers hearing their own voices is a boost to their memories, growth involvement, and egos.

Yet today, in all groups from kindergarten on, silent individual work consumes most of the time. The only voice to be exercised is the teacher's.

Not only is this the hangover from early research on silent reading; it is also the result of too much hyperactivity on the part of today's youngsters. Teachers use workbooks, skill devices, and all varieties of "games" and gadgets to "keep the kids busy, quiet, and under control." To a degree, such concern is not idle. Many teachers with too many volatile or emotionally disturbed youngsters admit their major efforts must be spent in keeping all safe—only once in a while really teaching. Critics might be enlightened to visit classrooms, especially in urban areas. From beginning to upper grades one feels the tension and must wonder "How can a teacher stand this day after day?"

Yet, youngsters in their beginning reading days need to hear, to hear themselves, to *see and say* words, news items, stories. Even we adults, hearing new names and words, like to see and repeat them. Multiple-sensory approaches, especially when accompanied with satisfying feelings, boost learning and make it stick. The early days of orally chanting spelling lessons and group oral reading helped many, especially the less avid, to learn how to read and how to spell. When this was combined with help in writing, the basis for continued growth was built.

Once Over Lightly—Not Enough Repetition

The third neglected observation is another hangover of yesterday. It is the fear of repetition, practice, and drill. I can recall being bored by the singsong repetition of the multiplication tables. Yet, today I can recall every item with ease. That was the day when *everybody* did the same thing at the same time. Teaching individuals and small groups makes possible the ability to give those who need much repetition a chance to get it. The danger of boring the rest of the class is thus obviated. For the past decades, the word "drill" has become a shame word. No matter what it is called, repetition in an interesting way is essential now as then so that boys and girls can latch onto and hold items and elements in memory—for keeps.

These three lacks—lack of proper observance of regular daily attendance, lack of more oral experiences in the daily programs, and lack of adequate practice, repetition, or drill—contribute to the failure of youngsters to become readers, especially the less verbal. Pressures on teachers to give a position of priority to the skills will not affect students whose reading loss is affected by these three common lacks. And, the reform necessary, unlike most reforms, could be without additional cost to the schools!

BASIC REMEDIES NEEDED

Home, school, and community must exercise their obligation to improve attendance. This involves an attitude about the importance of school from the first day in kindergarten. Publicity in local press, radio, and TV is easily obtainable. School letters to parents can be made effective. Daily recognition and concern on the part of every teacher is a must. Also, every teacher needs to plan carefully and carry out a method of reinducting the absentee upon his or her return. This can best be done in a group in which a spirit of helpfulness and concern is a regular part of daily work.

Becky, absent for a week with a serious infection, received the cheerful "Welcome back, Becky" in a chant. On a chart on the board was listed:

This Week's Helpers — Sandra — Math
George — Reading
Kip — Spelling
Alice — School Activities

These third graders got a frequent lesson in the importance of daily attendance and sequential learning by aiding those who had to miss school. The absentee was also aided in the adjustments demanded upon the return.

A whole volume should be written on this one topic—the importance of regular attendance at school. Once neglect from any source has dampened a youngster's "willingness to go to school" a dangerous progression may be the result, reading interests may drop, a child may sense a lack, and truancy may begin for some.

LET THEIR VOICES BE HEARD

A sixth-grade teacher in an urban area was assigned a group of nineteen boys and twelve girls, all seemingly more mature than twelve or thirteen years, full of bawdy talk, rough play, and a defiant attitude toward the teacher. The teacher was presented to the class by the principal: "Miss X. is an *A* teacher. She'll make you learn." Miss X., in her third year of teaching, had ideas. She said, "I hate *to be made* to do something. But I like to do things I like to do. Together, we can do things we like—maybe a surprise for Mr. P., the principal, and all the rest. Like a play we write, or a story we sing—something we'll like." One boy, who turned out to be a leader, quieted the rest and said, "Give us a show how." She said OK, opened a book and said, "This is in the latest book—it's not in your school's library. Maybe no one in school has read it or heard this." She read from a new book, her own, a poem "Mother to a Son," by Langston Hughes.* The group calmed down as she read. Then Pete, the leader, said, "Is there more in there?" "Yes, do you want another poem? This first is by one of our great black poets." Next, she read "Jake Hates All The Girls" by E.E. Cummings.** The kids roared.

A new relationship was growing between teacher and group. And, to the surprise of the principal and other teachers, this group asked to appear on their weekly assembly as a voice choir, chanting "Jake Hates All The Girls." From this experience came added interest, first in reading "jazzy" things, then in skill development.

Their motivation was probably initiated by sensing that this new teacher regarded them as real. Her work had been influenced by *36 Children,**** a book about one teacher's experience in teaching children from the ghetto, which she read in her teacher preparation.

Keeping youngsters of any age busy with individual "stuff" so they are quiet and orderly prevents them from getting truly stirred into constructive actions and getting fired with a real eagerness to learn. Not only is this nonproductive for the pupils, it also prevents the growth of creativity, inventiveness, and imagination on the part of the teacher.

MOTIVATION—DEVELOPING SELF-STARTERS

The key to anyone's successful learning is motivation. What we really want to do, we do! We are willing to put forth effort, to struggle, to overcome some defeats—but we stick with it. A perfect example of this is the ten-month-old infant who can crawl rapidly, but now wants to walk. He or she pulls up against a chair, flops down hard, but immediately gets up and tries again. There may be days of actually hard work, a few unaided steps, more falls, and at last success! Walking! So with block building, or water play, or riding a tricycle. There is an urge, real attention, energy output—and achievement. This is the simple formula for working our way through life. The germ or key is the inner desire, "I want to read by myself." Good counsellors who work with individuals, one at a time, search for what makes each tick.

---

*Nancy Larrick, ed., *Crazy to Be Alive in Such a Strange World* (New York: M. Evans, 1977).
**Ibid.
***Herbert Kohl, *36 Children* (New York: New American Library, 1968).

A conscientious teacher of any age group considers this inspiring of each youngster essential. It is not easy to develop, however. Some may have desires but bent in the wrong direction. In pre-service education helping teachers to acquire competence in this area should have high priority.

The effects of early experiences before entering school are apparent. Those who enter wide-eyed, able to talk and listen, eager to try out everything, have the privileged seed of fitness for continued growth in reading, in all skills, in all learning.

PHONICS

In our United-States-bandwagon approach, once some of our public grabbed the idea that Johnny couldn't read because by some conspiracy teachers refused to teach him phonics, a veritable wave of phonic plans, ideas, and materials was washed up on the school's doorstep. One program demanded that all books and all printed materials be kept away from preschoolers and beginners until the youngsters had mastered a set of rules about phonics. Some children who already could read were pronounced not-yet-ready for reading because they did not do well with the rules. In one community, a committee of investigators charged that the school failed to teach phonics. The teachers held demonstration lessons in phonics and displayed their phonic materials, but they used the term *word study* instead of phonics. In an interview with a young teacher, a principal asked, "Can you teach decoding?" The young gal asked, "Do you mean phonics?" The principal said, "No, I mean the latest—decoding." She was not selected. A book, "Fun About Phonics," should be written about the ignorance and quackery that has been aroused by such an everyday need—phonics.

Believe it or not, there once was a booklet called *Phonics or No Phonics*. I read it and found the author left the question open-ended. This was the era when the see-and-say, no phonics (or only bootleg phonics) swept the schools. In this age of new inventions and areas with new vocabularies, of foreign names and places and important names in news events, how would we adults manage without phonics?

Granted, our English language is not as phonically consistent as is Italian or Spanish. And we insist upon keeping the *thoughs, throughs,* and *enoughs*. According to some specialists, approximately seventy-five percent of our words are spelled as they sound. For them, a reader needs phonics to become an agile reader.

Again, close acquaintance with an alert four- or five-year-old who is already showing eagerness to read will hear him sounding out Babar and making jingles, ''Bud, bud, fell in the mud.'' An ABC book read by child and adult has many opportunities for fun with phonics. A peppy young mother related to a group of kindergarten mothers how her young Andy came to read already ''chiefly by having fun with our ABC book. He'd bombed the *B*'s and sizzled the *Z*'s. Then he'd enjoyed mouthing all the letters. So it went from there to trying out the sounds of words he noticed.'' The book he'd enjoyed was *ABC of Babar.**

Children at five range in phonic experiences from no association of sound and symbol, or even an awareness of this mental trick, to those who are already ''sounding out'' words by themselves. A wise teacher takes his or her clues from the youngsters. The daily program includes help with common sounds, words, and letters when needed in the reading of names, labels, notices, and news events. Some who listen catch on; some, not ready, tend to their work. Individual differences must be met. Many phonics materials are produced for kindergarten and primary grades. However, the use of commercial games and exercises, if used, should not be overly stressed.

TESTING FOR UNDERSTANDING AND PLANNING NEXT STEPS

An array of tests for school beginners is now extant. Each has strong advocates and requires sensible use and intelligent interpretation. Each does focus on an individual child: if properly used, tests help teachers to get a more personal acquaintance with the room full of five-year-olds. The emphasis on predicting rather than understanding seems to keep growing, however. Parents frequently are given pangs over the reading-readiness test when used to separate the ''ready'' from the ''unready.''

To a veteran teacher, the fallacy of predicting has been met too frequently to be discarded as ''just an accident.'' Five-year-old Harry, kept in kindergarten two years because he ''did poorly'' on the

*Jean de Brunhoff, *ABC of Babar* (New York: Random House, 1969).

reading-readiness test, became a basketball center in high school, not one scholastic failure, is now a sophomore in college, and hopes to become a forester; Mary Ellen, a pixie-looking five-year-old smiled readily but talked little, declared "slow" on two tests, won an award as a volunteer in a hospital, is now a freshman doing well in college, and hopes to become a dietitian. Both had encouraging parents. Both had to overcome the effects of the two teachers who "played God" with test scores. There is now, very properly, great interest in longitudinal studies of behavior. With information over a long period of time, interpreting scores and all early symptoms and symbols will become a more reliable practice.

There are some key elements in the behavior of preschoolers and kindergartners that do reveal some indications in a general way. Even with these indications, though, caution is wise. The human creation is too complex in this unpredictable age for anyone to play the role of a prophet or prophetess.

LITERATE SCHOOL ENVIRONMENT

A casual walk through a school, its halls, and classrooms can indicate the inclusiveness of the reading goals. In the corridors, signs, invitations to classroom activities, tables and shelves with books for browsing while waiting, displays of creative effort—all reveal something of the ongoing life in the school. The classrooms get one closer to children's work and also each classroom climate. One sees memos regarding committee responsibilities, some written by youngsters, displays of projects on tables and shelves, books, and skill materials. A daily program, often in the center for all to see, is also an indicator of the group's life.

Especially revealing is the library. What are the come-hither displays, how much child participation is evident, how many individuals and groups in the library, what evidences that the library functions as a research center for individuals and groups on projects of personal or group interests, or science and social studies projects?

In one school, a reading corner outside the principal's office, with books for children and adults, was kept in order and up to date by a committee of primary and intermediate grade children. The sign "Read While You Wait," also made by youngsters, was prominently placed. As I visited, this was revealed to be a truly literate school. Reading functioned as an integral part of the entire school. Children talked excitedly about their favorite books, authors, and illustrators from first grade on. They also interrogated me about my preferences. And most amazing, a number protested the high prices of today's books. In a school in the same community, when I asked fourth graders what they thought of the cost of books today, one boy immediately said, "Nothing. The school doesn't have to pay for books." This chap probably will be active in some cut-the-school-budget taxpayers' club.

The major goal in teaching reading, namely to develop independent, functional, and critical readers, is apparent in a visit on a regular day, not on a special occasion. The individual and group guidance toward this goal is essential. It just doesn't happen to the majority without teachers' judicious efforts. Some guidelines for such efforts are presented in the following chapter.

CHAPTER 4

The Reading Program—
Which Direction?

"I AM LEARNING HOW TO READ," WAS KINKY-HAIRED DIANE'S excited report to her grandmother on her first trip home from kindergarten. "Already?" asked grandmother. "Sure! I look for my name all over where it says Diane. Now I can read Diane." This kindergarten teacher printed first names of all children on cards and tacked them at eye-level about the room. Those who already could read their names could collect their name cards and store them in their lockers, over which each one's name already had been placed. Nine children responded, an important clue to the teacher.

In this school, the entire staff guided all children to become *functional* readers rather than readers who "learned how to read." To achieve this major educational goal, five functional goals were kept in sight on the teacher's desk, on bulletin boards, on a placard in the waiting space outside the principal's office—and in the teacher's lunchroom! Let's face it, the minutia of daily routines for a group of any age can blur larger goals into oblivion. In this school, the principal was a realist. The teachers nicknamed him "Lest We Forget," because of his constant reminding them, or interrogating them, about why we teach reading. The answer "So they learn to read" was taboo. Read for what? Why? When?

FIVE MAJOR READING GOALS

These five goals might fittingly be kept in sight on every teacher's desk:

—Guide pupils to know *when* it is essential and to their advantage to read, both in and out of school.

—Guide pupils to know how *to select* what to read.

—Guide pupils *to read skillfully* what is selected in relation to its use.

—Guide pupils *to appraise critically* the content in terms of its intended use.

—Guide pupils in using ideas gained from reading.

GUIDE PUPILS TO KNOW WHEN TO READ

Often the first goal is assumed to be functioning in many classroom situations. Pupils read when the daily schedule says "Reading—9:15 to 10:00." This daily dose of reading as an assigned lesson, often having no goal other than a satisfactory grade on the daily lesson, may be an important contributing factor to the lack of functional reading in so many of our "schooled" adults. True, practice in reading is needed in order to acquire and improve reading skill. A pupil needs to see the *value* in reading, the value in terms of living better and more happily, not in terms of getting good grades, being promoted, or having his or her name at the top of a class list. Then even practice makes sense. There needs to be guidance in becoming aware of occasions when it is not only an advantage to read, but many varied experiences in which children read and realize the pleasure and value in being able to read.

A discerning teacher sees that not only the whole school environment but especially the curriculum must be so planned to offer opportunities to deal with items, problems, and individual and group long-range experiences. A vigorous, functional program of reading demands a vigorous functional curriculum—one in which pupils are guided in becoming increasingly sensitive to their persistent problems, and one in which they grow through the use of adequate study to arrive at acceptable solutions to their problems. They will learn when to kill time by reading a story; when to go to a book for information; when to read poetry; when to use the encyclopedia, maps, and graphs; when to consult more than one reference book; when to refer to newspapers, magazines, and current materials and when to read for other purposes. They will, of course, learn to recognize when to read and reread in order to improve their skill and to probe real meanings.

It is a part of *every* teacher's responsibility to help pupils to know when to use reading for added pleasure during recreation, to extend their knowledge, to test the correctness of their ideas, to learn which course of action is preferable, and to gain other helps. It would be timely if many adults also might have such guidance.

In an informal experiment twelve able fifth- and sixth-grade pupils, who read a sketchy description of "How to Balance an Aquarium," were asked if they had gotten enough information to guide them in making a balanced aquarium; they answered "yes" in unison. These pupils who had had a narrow reading background did not sense the inadequacy of the knowledge they had gained. Knowing when to read for more information is of utmost importance if pupils are to be thorough in their study at six, ten, eighteen—or forty-two.

GUIDE PUPILS TO KNOW HOW TO SELECT WHAT TO READ

It is obvious that a person wanting to find a telephone number would not be successful if he or she searched for it in a cookbook; nor would a girl searching for information on the latest jet plane be satisfied if she chose a book about airplanes copyrighted in 1933; nor would a sixth-grade boy seeking a story of western adventure accept a book of fairy tales. The selection of what to read is of considerable importance to purposeful reading.

Although frequent concern has been expressed over the "lowbrow" taste of adults, the relation of their selection to the failure of giving them an opportunity to select in school is all too often overlooked. This was the responsibility of those who planned the quality of the reading program. Part of the failure may be attributed to the spoon-feeding resulting from a textbook-conditioned curriculum. A classroom needs to be equipped with a variety of books, magazines, newspapers, pictorial materials, films, and cassettes, and there should also be access to a good school library and public library.

Merely the availability of sufficient materials, however, will not ensure the development of wise selection. Teachers must give adequate guidance in terms of the ability of each pupil and the nature of his or her reason for reading. Furthermore, the teacher needs to know, as far as possible, what the pupils are reading voluntarily out of school, since such reading can be more indicative of individual preferences than in-school choices. At an early age, children will reveal preferences; what they choose to read adds to our understanding of them.

GUIDE PUPILS TO READ SKILLFULLY

The major part of teaching effort in the primary grades, and frequently in the intermediate grades, is directed toward teaching pupils how to acquire or improve their ability to read the materials of their respective grades. Stress is placed on such basic skills as word recognition, word meaning, and sentence and paragraph understanding, which are necessary in comprehension. The importance attached to acquiring and extending these abilities in reading is sound: a reader obviously must be able to get the author's idea from the symbols on the page.

Word recognition requires the development of a number of techniques of which phonics (or decoding) is very important. The eyes must pause long enough to see the letters, their sound-in-sequence must then register mentally and, if the reading is oral, must be vocalized. This sounds like a simple process, but it is full of hazards for some beginners. The greatest amount of materials to develop skills has been produced to help teachers get youngsters over the hurdles in this process. But reading in today's challenging, problem-solving curriculum requires additional techniques. For example, when a first-grade pupil reads the notes of the first grade in the school paper, he or she not only wants to know "what they say," but reacts to them. Do they include items that were important? Were some more important items omitted? Any errors? Comprehension here involves more than the ability to pronounce each word and to give back the content; it means considering the ideas and dealing with them in a reflective manner. All the separate skills necessary to develop this type of comprehension are included in the goal of teaching pupils to be *skillful* readers.

When the program for beginning readers emphasizes phonics and other word recognition techniques to the minimization or neglect of comprehension and the function of reading, the result is what one would expect, the lack of adequate comprehension in the later grades. No doubt the almost fanatic emphasis on phonics has contributed to the later poor grades on reading comprehension tests. Certainly, reading to "recite," which I have called the "spit-back" method, fails to develop the critical comprehension demanded in life's experiences. This point will be developed in the next goal.

GUIDE PUPILS TO KNOW HOW TO APPRAISE THE CONTENT IN TERMS OF ITS INTENDED USE

In discussing which story would be a good one for the first grade to read at a Christmas party, one boy suggested "The Three Bears." Immediately his suggestion was opposed by several who said, "That is not a Christmas story." Actually, these pupils were appraising stories in terms of their intended use. A story about beavers written to entertain may have value as story reading but may not serve to enlighten pupils who are making a study of the wild fur-bearing animals of their locality and want to find an accurate description of the life of a beaver.

Critical appraisal at times must take into consideration the copyright date of the story, the author's knowledge of the subject, and his purpose in writing the story. In addition, it involves the ability to check elements of the content with previously accepted facts. Critical appraisal, therefore, is the acceptance of what meets with the reader's approval, or the nonacceptance or rejection of ideas that are out of date, sound false, or do not bear on the purpose of reading. It needs to be stated here again that the curriculum must be organized around challenging experiences. In the study pertaining to these enterprises, the pupils read and select or reject what they read in terms of its qualities and its bearing on their purpose.

Until these later years, the complex and deep process of comprehension has not received the attention of reading specialists. Not too long ago, any attempt to probe this aspect of reading was considered trespassing on the psychology of *thinking*—and this was psychologists' territory. Fortunately, this erroneous division of the mental process of reading no longer exists.

Stuart Chase gave me the most helpful reference on comprehension in his book, *Guides to Straight Thinking.** It includes such common errors as making faulty generalizations and our either-or logic. More will be included later on the emphasis on either-or logic in workbooks and tests, a negative influence that extends into adults' thinking.

---

*Stuart Chase, *Guides to Straight Thinking, with Thirteen Common Fallacies* (New York: Harper & Row, 1956).

At the age of six or seven, many children are able to read and say, "Not all dogs have long, bushy tails." The inclusion of guidance in thinking straight is essential in reading contemporary news, and listening to radio and TV. A child who is startled by an item he or she hears may ask, "Who said that?" then add, "Why would he say that?" comments that indicate this child is thinking.

Whenever I dwell on comprehension I am reminded of the beginning of the Frank Jennings' preface in his book on reading: "Teaching is the most dangerous profession. It deals with our children, the most precious of our natural resources. It refines them into brave and wonderful adults or it grossly degrades them into dull, over-aged adolescents." *

GUIDE PUPILS TO KNOW HOW TO USE IDEAS GAINED FROM READING

Ideas gained from reading may be understood and remembered, but not acted upon. A group of fifth-grade pupils who had been reading about the development of oil resources in Alaska planned to paint a mural on an unused chalkboard in their classroom to depict their new knowledge of Alaska. In the preliminary plans, the pupils reverted to the "igloo concept" of Eskimo life, not utilizing the information gained from their reading until the teacher called their attention to this fact. We frequently notice the lack of connection between *knowing* and *acting upon knowing*. "You know better" is a common expression, not only of teachers, but of relatives and friends. Teaching should be directed toward guiding pupils to use what they learn from reading—to carry over into practice the knowledge they have gained from reading. We need to help them make this a habit.

In order to help growing youngsters to act-on-knowing, many experiences are needed, some of which make them aware of the "erroneous and hypocritical" logic we adults all too often use. The teaching of reading often found in even up-to-date schools has become so removed from daily living that one teacher commented, "Just today, I discovered, thanks to my kids, the connection between being honest and using what you get from reading." Yet all of us have heard or said, "He preaches one thing, but practices another." During our political

---

*Frank E. Jennings, *This Is Reading* (New York: Bureau of Publications, Teachers College, Columbia University, 1965).

campaigns, the air is literally full of such examples. Yet, an inclusive set of reading goals can and should affect not only the quality of the reader, but also subsequent behavior.

These five goals need to be in the forefront of the teacher's mind in teaching reading, in guiding even the youngest children. It is essential to put great emphasis on them to change the too long held teaching of ''reading to give back'' to reading to find out, to explore, to enjoy, to react to, and to use.

CHAPTER 5

What Do We Mean—Phonics?

IN A PUBLIC MEETING RECENTLY AN IRATE PARENT ROSE AND SAID, "I'm going to make a pronouncement! We are not going to improve the reading scores in this school until we make phonics the main part of our reading program!" The chairperson, a tolerant individual, asked, "Have you any specifics?" Her response was, "Never mind specifics! Phonics is phonics! Everybody knows what that means." And she received fairly good applause—in a so-called "enlightened" community.

In spite of the now hackneyed defenses of teachers' efforts in teaching phonics, it seems desirable to present some ABC's about phonics before continuing details about teaching reading in the elementary school.

In learning to read, children meet a more complicated function of language than they do in learning to speak. In reading, they come upon symbols called letters, arranged in sequence in words that represent meanings. To get at the meaning, they must be able to translate the letters into sounds, so that they can identify the words they stand for. When they see the word *free,* they must translate the letters into an *fr* and *ee* sound, then blend them and sound out *free*. When they do this, they are using phonics.

Phonics is the term commonly used for the process of translating individual letters and combinations of letters into sounds that identify the word they represent. In oral reading, the word is pronounced; in silent reading, it is heard in inner intellectual recesses. If a child recognizes the word *free* from some previous experience without sounding it out, we say he or she has learned it "by sight." Through either phonics or sight, he or she eventually recognizes the word with ease and ultimately with the seeming "unawareness" that adult readers reveal. By looking at word after word after word, a child ultimately grows in the speedy recognition of words.

Two fields are pertinent in gaining a more adequate understanding of the child's acquisition of phonics as an aid to his or her reading. The first is the nature of phonics as inherent in written English, and the second, the way in which a young child tends to learn. The casual observer needs a degree of understanding of both in order to avoid oversimplification or quackery.

An examination of only some of the irregularities, inconsistencies, and complexities found in the spelling-to-sound relationship in English words follows. Its purpose is to help us recognize the burden carried by a young child in first sounding out words. A complete phonetic or linguistic analysis of English words would make up a comprehensive volume. The vignette presented here, however, will highlight the problem faced by a child in his first contacts with printed English words and will help us to be more realistic and understanding about his frustrations and bewilderment. It will also—it is hoped—challenge the soundness of the theorists who believe that an all-phonic approach to beginning reading should be the heaven-sent manna for all children.

A LOOK AT VOWELS—THEIR REGULARITY AND VAGARIES

Our alphabet of twenty-six letters is made up of five vowels, *a, e, i, o, u* (and *y* when it is sounded as *i*), and nineteen consonants. The vowels are produced in an easy, flowing manner, without the nearly explosive or forceful pressure required in sounding consonants such as *b, d,* and *p.* Vowel-sounds are subtle to the young listener's ear. Indeed, some of the variations are too subtle for most adult ears to detect. Only phoneticians and others experienced in speech have such competence. Many dictionaries, for example, ascribe eight variations to the sound of *a,* from *ā* as in *cāke* to *à* as in *sofà.* Some linguists have analyzed the language and have discovered more than forty sounds of *a*!

The standard sounds of vowels vary according to their use in words. Knowing when *a* sounds *ä* or *ă* or *ā*, or is silent as in *fēar*, presents a problem that those deeply concerned with the teaching of phonics should pause to examine. The rules are neither few nor simple.

One of the most regular sound-symbol rules that a child acquires in his reading career is that a vowel is usually long* or says its name, when it occurs in a short one-syllable word that ends in a silent *e*. Such words as *cake, pole,* and *bike* are consistent with this rule. To understand it, a youngster must have learned previously that a syllable is a collection of letters that blend into one sound—like *ate, be,* and *ing*. He will also need to feel at home with the idea of one-syllable and two-or-more-syllable words. In addition, he must have acquired the auditory acuity to hear the *ā* sound as distinguished from other sounds. Children with hearing problems commonly reveal their handicap in their efforts to identify vowel sounds.

One rule for short vowels, though apparently simple, also requires specific learnings: A vowel is usually short when it is in a short word or syllable ending with a consonant, such as *făt* and *bĭt*. The short words will obviously be easier for children to manage than the two-syllable words. They may quickly notice that *fat* is a short word ending in *t*, which is a consonant; therefore the *a* sounds *ă*.

The two-syllable word *bitten* places a heavier burden on children because they must be aware of the proper place to divide the word into two syllables: *bit* and *ten*. Teachers and reading specialists commonly defer work on methods of syllabification until children are beyond the beginning-reading period, even though the children frequently meet words to which this rule applies. The rules about when vowels are long and when short, however, might be considered "merely the beginning."

Enter the Vowel Digraphs

In many common words in the English language, two or more vowels are used together. They often present a real stumbling block to both child and teacher, because those that are exceptions to the rule are almost as common as those that fit the rule. One general rule is that when two vowels are together, the first is given the long sound and the

---

Long and *short* are used in this work to indicate the *ā* and *ă*, or *ē* and *ĕ*, or the sounds of other letters.

second is silent. Words like *tāil* and *bēat* fit the rule, but everyday words like *does* and *hour* do not. Some exceptions are so frequent that rules for them have been created. Many of us still recall at times the spelling aid "*I* before *e* except after *c* or when sounded as *a* as in *neighbor* and *weigh*." In some words, the first vowel is short and the second, silent, as in *health* and *weather*. Vowels are also influenced when used with certain consonants, especially *r*. The *i* in *girl*, the *o* in *work*, and the *e* in *her* take on special sounds that are neither long nor short.

The sound of vowels is affected also by the point at which the accent falls in a word. As a rule, in a two-syllable word, the vowel in the accented syllable is long. The one in the other syllable is given the slight or indistinct sound called *schwa*, as in *brōken*, *hīking*, and *dāred*—but not always. Words like *water* and *began* do not follow this pronunciation principle.

The intention here is not to present the rules that govern the sounds of vowels used singly or in combinations in words. Instead, this brief examination of vowels is intended to remind those of us who recognize words automatically of the problem vowels present to a child learning to read English especially if it is through an "all-phonic" approach.

CONSONANTS

Consonants are simpler to pronounce than vowels are. To begin with, most consonants demand more physical action in being sounded than do the vowels. Children can actually feel themselves pronounce *b*, *m*, *z*, and *d*—especially at the beginning and end of words. Most consonants are fairly consistent in their sounds, and, therefore, to the child they seem more "reliable" than vowels. However, one consonant, *c*, is particularly fickle. In certain uses, *c* takes on the soft sound of *s*; in others, the hard sound of *k*. A child often starts to pronounce such words as *cent, city,* and *certain* with the hard sound of *k*, as in *care, car,* and *come*. Dwight, a serious youngster in third grade who loved to read after a slow start, came upon the word *certain*. He first pronounced it *curtain*, then realized that made no sense. He said, "Who made up this spelling? He's stupid." (Shades of George Bernard Shaw!)

Some consonants must seem like useless additions to words, not only because they are silent but also because it would be almost impossible to pronounce them in the words if they were not silent. It must seem to a reasonable child like Dwight that such words as *ought, catch,* and *gnome* are foolishly spelled. Children enjoy exploding the *b* at the end of *dumb,* the *h* in *ghost,* and the *k* in *knew.* No wonder people of far less note than George Bernard Shaw have argued for a revision of spelling in order to remove some of the gross dislocations between symbols and their respective sounds.

Consonant Blends and Digraphs

Although consonants do present less variation of sound, and therefore fewer complications, to the young reader, the nature of the sounding-out difficulty they cause should not be glossed over. Notice the variety of consonant blends in a short list of everyday words:

bread	drive	grew	scream	snore
blew	flew	place	skin	spell
clear	free	prize	slip	stir
crab	glad	scat	smog	swat

Each blend has its own sound. A child may understand the sound of *b* in *big* and *r* in *ray* but struggle to sound *br* in *bread.* So with every consonant blend. Each demands of the child its distinctive sound.

When two consonants are used in pairs known as digraphs, they may cause a more serious stumbling block to the child than consonant blends do. In the blends, the letters maintain a semblance of their characteristic sound when their sounds are smoothed together. In consonant digraphs, neither letter keeps its sound identity. The following words illustrate this fact of phonics.

photo	where	shall	cheap	the
phonics	why	she	chair	this

No wonder Dick, who was a poor speller, included words such as these in a list he titled "Phoolisch werds."

There are many more cases in which sounds deviate from normal expectations, especially to a beginner or a less experienced reader—or to a child (or even an adult) not versatile in the English language.

Imagine the amount of explanation needed to give the reasons underlying pronunciation of *one, son, sun, upon, no, not,* and *on.* These examples are high on word lists used in books for beginners. If their recognition and oral pronunciation were to be taught solely via phonics, pity the teacher and the children.

AND STILL MORE: SYLLABIFICATION AND ACCENT OR STRESS

Early in a child's reading career, he meets the word *syllable,* which, according to definition, means "those letters in a word that, when taken together, make one sound." Words of two or more syllables are readily spoken by children—and some are also quickly recognized in print. *Christmas, Halloween,* and *birthday* are commonly recognized and clearly pronounced by children even before they have heard the word *syllable.* They notice that some words are long and are pronounced sound after sound. The rules for syllabification, however, are commonly deferred until after the third grade.

Many young readers acquire considerable awareness of syllables through their discovery of common suffixes. One class of first-graders changed the simple jingle "I can ring, I can sing, I can swing," to "I am ringing, I am singing, I am swinging." Following the discovery that they could add the suffix *ing* to these three words, they extended the list to include *playing, eating, sleeping,* and *working.*

The suffix *ed* would not lend itself to such easy discovery as did *ing.* I can play could be changed to *I played,* but *I can eat* would be followed by *I ate.* The high frequency of irregular verbs adds to the complexity of learning correct English usage. No wonder that many who acquire English as a second language find it difficult. A teacher who is aware of the irregular qualities in our English language is quick to sense when children's explorations will lead to the discovery of a general pattern or rule and when they may highlight irregular forms and word structures.

Children, for example, can understand suffixes and can see the function of word endings such as *ing, ed,* and *es.* But in their early attempts to use them, especially in spelling, they quickly meet a variety of regulations and exceptions. "I did pay for my milk," wrote Gerald to his teacher. "Yes he payed it," wrote Cynthia, who was the class bookkeeper. Rules for when to drop the final *e* and when to double the final consonant before adding a suffix cannot usually be acquired until the children become mature enough to assimilate such regulations. Before that time, though, they can learn to be ready for the unexpected. This is particularly true when they write and must spell.

In sounding out polysyllabic words, one must learn where to place the accent if the word is to be pronounced acceptably. This aspect of phonics usually is relegated to older children, those old enough to use a dictionary. This is reasonable. A child often is in a quandary about where to place the accent or stress when he meets a word in reading that he does not commonly hear or use. One rule—namely, that in two-syllable words, the accent is usually on the first syllable—can be understood by the younger readers. Emphasis on this seems unnecessary, however; most of the words a child recognizes in his reading convey to him the pronunciation to which he is accustomed. It is when his reading vocabulary begins to extend beyond his listening vocabulary that the pronunciation of new words may require a knowledge of rules and of accent placement, and the use of a dictionary.

WORD MEANING AND PRONUNCIATION

Some words we call *homonyms* take their pronunciation from their meaning in the sentence. The word *tear* in the sentences "I shall *tear* the paper along this line," and "I saw a *tear* roll down his cheek" are examples of this added irregularity. A thoughtful reader who, when reading orally, pronounces *read* as *rĕd* instead of *rēad* discovers his error. The relatively large number of homonyms occurring in the child's everyday writing call for special attention in teaching spelling. Here, spelling in relation to meaning must be acquired. When a child asks, "How do you spell *here*?" an alert adult asks. "How are you using it?" or says, "Tell me what you wish to write."

Whose Pronunciation Is Correct?

Those who travel in the United States and who listen attentively will still notice pronunciation characteristics indigenous to particular areas, although TV and radio are lessening this. They will hear a man discuss his *"idear"* in Maine and his *"īdē"* in southern Missouri. They will meet far more *äh* sounds in the South than in the Dakotas, and will surely notice the slighting of *g* by North Carolinians describing their *"workin', runnin',* and *playin'."* Many of these geographical speech characteristics are still accepted. Some, however, like the *dis* for *this* and *ting* for *thing* stemming from the German influence in some mid-western sections are not accepted. In general, however, phoneticians and linguists are tolerant about the liberties taken in pronunciation. Proof of such tolerance can be found in any dictionary that includes several pronunciations for a large number of words.

When Junior Asks, "What's This Word?"

The foregoing brief account of the irregularities of vowels and consonants, of vowel digraphs and consonant digraphs, of silent and schwa sounds should at least alert us to the nature of the problem that faces beginning readers and their teachers. When a child asks, "What's this word?" an adult informed in the variation of letter sounds will not say, "Sound out the letters." Instead, a helpful parent might say "Spell it out. Then I can tell you what the word is." In the beginning period, some youngsters can read before they know all the letters. With them, when they ask for help, it is best to say, "Show me the word."

DIRECT TEACHING

When youngsters in first grade and later grades meet words that give them difficulty, but words that lend themselves to learning an element of phonics, time should be taken to teach whatever that element is. For example, adding an *s* to make a word plural is a need quite common to the first grade. Most commercial lists of sequential lessons, unless developed via many examples of their occurrence in familiar words, may be time-consuming and irrelevant to some of the group. A teacher, therefore, needs to keep tuned-in to the needs as they arise.

Some surprises occur. In one first grade, Phil and Phyllis enjoyed the teacher's comment, "Here are two names that start with a real phonics clinker." Although no other *ph* names or words were met, the youngsters, when reminded that *sure* sounded different from the way it was spelled, said, "Yes, like Phil and Phyllis." More suggestions will follow in later chapters.

Would that those who advocate an "all-phonics" program would read this chapter.

CHAPTER **6**

A Room Full of Fives

FIVE-YEAR-OLD CHILDREN IN KINDERGARTEN REVEAL MANY differences in background. Some are energetic talkers, ready at all times to tell something, to enter discussion, and to respond to questions; others are "mummers," too shy to utter even monosyllables, often not even free enough to nod assent, and sometimes actually frightened at being spoken to.

There are, of course, a number of children between these two extremes, and also many variations in the oral language ability of those who talk. Some may have had rich experiences in the home and neighborhood; through the experiences of travel, TV, and radio, they have acquired a large, meaningful vocabulary that can be used with rhythmic fluency and dramatic quality. Others who have had the most meager surroundings may have remained insensitive to some of the experiences possible even in their limited environment. Several children may be emotionally maladjusted because of home influence—overnurtured and therefore dependent and seemingly two to three years younger than they really are, or insecure and requiring constant personal assurance and encouragement at first to be happy. Many in the group may lack the ability to get along with their companions.

Some may have spoken only a foreign language in the home and may not be able to understand the simplest directions in English. As travel increases, more children of different language backgrounds and customs will enter our schools.

The most frequent comment of today's kindergarten teachers is,

"Many are very restless and have not learned to listen to directions." This higher volatility is a reflection of today's high-pressure age. Also, many of these youngsters were "kept under control" at home by hours of sitting before TV. They have not experienced the kind of day balanced with constructive and physically active work that wise teachers plan. As one fine, mature teacher said, "It takes time to get some of these kids in a calm enough condition to be fit to learn." Quite a contrast from the day when I became a teacher. Then, most young children and even oldsters had to be encouraged to become active and assertive. Others who have watched TV by the hours may reveal undeveloped abilities, no previous experiences in building, drawing, browsing in books, or creative play. This side of their development has been stilled while being stuffed with TV programs, only a few planned for a child.

These differences are obvious and provision must be made for them in the daily program if each child is to progress satisfactorily and develop to the utmost of his and her capacities, not only in reading but in all directions.

BOOKS—VARIED DAILY USE

Children who are just starting to recognize words and letters can share with the whole class a story hour in which a child selects a book for the teacher to read. For many, this may be a new experience; there is no reading of any kind to them in their homes. For them, the selection of which book to be read may of itself be a valuable learning experience. To others, this may be a continuation of a delightful time in day-care center, nursery school, and home. Attractive books for browsing, frequently changed, should be kept on a table so that the children can page through them. Browsing and looking at pictures spark interest and add to the needed growth in wanting to read. Children may take turns in selecting a book from this collection. With encouragement, some may tell why they made their choice, what the story seems to be about, and which pictures appeal to them.

The collection of books, changed from day to day, should be varied from ABC to simple stories and easy-to-read books in science and other books interesting to this age. The proper daily use of book browsing and the "storytime" are invaluable elements in the reading program for children at this beginning level. They are acquiring or adding to their awareness of reading and enjoyment through books.

Some who have come from an unliterary, meager background fairly zoom when given contacts with books, or when they hear stories read and are given a chance to react to this new experience in their lives. Unfortunately, there still are situations in which early labeling of children takes place and the seemingly less mature are committed to games, gadgets, and play, and denied the exposure through which they could really "catch up" with what they missed in earlier years.

IMPORTANT READING EVENTS

Another part of the early reading program is the use of experience charts and notices and news events. "Mr. Coombs comes today" was on the chart in the front of one room. Mr. Coombs was the science teacher in the school. He visited the kindergarten twice per week, chatted about science with the youngsters, and brought them interesting science materials to look at and explore, like shells, rocks, seedpods, and magnets. The first grade in this school made a list of *Signs of Autumn* which became "Our First Book in Science." They shared this with the kindergartners. Several of the eager beavers in the kindergarten then began making their own books.

Children's Observation as Teachers Write

In writing for children in kindergarten the use of white paper and black crayon or broad black pencil or flo-pen should be used so the letters and words look as nearly as possible like those in print. White on black, or chalkboard creates an optical illusion, making it harder for the youngsters to recognize letters from the chalkboard as the same as those in books.

A teacher who realizes the importance of including signs, memos, and notices finds innumerable occasions when they pop up. If the writing is "conversational," the teacher describes what he or she writes as it's being written; this has added value. Some youngsters may start to write as a result, they also have more specifics to associate with the form of a letter. The items written also can be better remembered.

When writing what children dictate, a teacher must be ready for some surprises. In answer to one teacher's suggestion that children dictate what she should remember to do, one—not the most alert lad—said, "Find out if they are selling toys from *Star Wars* at the five-and-ten."

Unlike the many exercises found in commercial materials, those from our-own-living materials have two advantages: first, they are based on the everyday vocabulary of the youngsters, and second, they help the child meet an obvious reason for reading. To non-English-speaking children, this latter is also helpful, just as an infant acquires his or her first words out of daily experiences.

EXPANDING THEIR WORLD

A teacher in a middle-economic area made a study of the traveling her twenty-seven youngsters had done. Nine had lived in different sections of the United States, two in foreign countries, sixteen had had trips on airplanes. None had had a trip on a train! Once the group had acquired a feeling for the regular day at school, a trip on a train was planned. The railroad, the parents, and the train crew cooperated. The trip was only a short run of thirty miles between two communities, but the event made a big impression. The day after the trip the children reported to the school principal: "That train went as fast as the fastest plane I was ever on." "This was more fun than going to Washington." "You can hardly see the houses and trees go by." And, most important, "When do we go on our next trip?"

New experiences, a trip to a dairybarn, the firehouse, the post office, and the bank help youngsters to assimilate innumerable bits of information, but more significantly, they stretch each child's concept of "my world," they make them wider-eyed, and they expand their ego. All of this occurs to the degree that the adults describe what's going on in simple language and give the youngsters lots of time to tell and retell what they saw. Vocabulary growth via good exposures of this kind naturally leaps ahead.

CAUTION—NO PRESSURE!

Any reference to young children's reading causes some professional educators to raise their hackles. "No reading in kindergarten!" This concern is rightly lodged against formal, everybody-does-or-fails programs. As a result of present-day concerns about low achievement in reading, such programs are increasing, often from parents' pressures. Some youngsters, however, suffer from the *absolutely no* reading as much as others suffer from the *prescribed* program. Just as a child learns to walk, talk, and notice symbols in a normal environment, he or she continues to learn from a rich school environment. Some of the learning is in reading if they are lucky enough to be in a literate school environment.

EVALUATION

There are many standardized tests available for use in kindergarten. Any one, if used to add to a teacher's understanding of each child, can have value. As cited in earlier chapters, tests when used not as an *absolute* but as an added item with which to observe each individual can be helpful. Their interpretation is safer if the teacher already has an acquaintance with a given child. For example, John, a young kindergartner, when taking a reading readiness test, used his crayons and made a colorful border of colored eggs around the entire page. The tester, a reading specialist, looked at this production and said to the teacher, "Tell me about this youngster." The teacher smiled and said, "He's really very bright. Can read quite well books for sevens and eights. Let's ask him to tell us about it." When John was asked to tell about his work, he said, "I didn't want to mark out all this dumb stuff so I made the whole page look good." Fortunately, John's teacher knew him.

Unfortunately, the cost of tests in money and time makes teachers and all test users add weight to their importance. The intelligent users who are aware of the test's reliability (if available) and the multiple factors that bear an influence on the learning or quality being measured are on the increase in today's schools.

CHAPTER 7

The Sixes: Their Multilevels in Reading

AS ONE FACES OLDER GROUPS, ONE FACTOR BECOMES INCREASINGLY obvious; the variations within the group, even if organized homogeneously, grow larger. We should rejoice over this realization because it proves the uniqueness and strength of individual personalities. If only the hankering for standardized-grade-level-kids could be permanently interred!

For years the classification of students by *grade level* has been the established terminology and practice. As a result, schools have been continually confronted with the need to label children's success in terms of this figment "grade level." Those above grade level were the "in" group, those below were "out." "To keep up to grade level" was—and still is, I fear—the major goal in all grades in all subjects.

Yet, all studies of children over the years have indicated their range of ability, some one or two years less mature at age six and others one or more years more mature. All were normal youngsters but with different responses to their daily experiences. To bring all up to the grade norm, which teachers are still not only advised to do and try to do desperately, is an impossibility. The waste of teachers' time and efforts on this is the least unfortunate part of the error. The major tragedy, and tragedy it is, is the oppressive effect on the children labeled "below grade."

THREE FUNCTIONAL READING LEVELS

From my contacts with children and schools, I have come to regard elementary-age youngsters in terms of their functional level. Beginners at five, who are in the kindergarten, can be classified as *First Functional Level*. At this first level the majority of fives reveal awareness of print, use of reading in some situations, and specific items like letters, words (some at sight, some with first steps in phonics), the front of the book, and the reading from left to right. All of this learning is accompanied by such a general statement as: a general eagerness to learn to read by himself. Therefore, this is properly described as functional.

The *Second Functional Level* is being approached when youngsters have acquired some adequacy in the use of word recognition techniques, including phonics, word cues, sight recognition, and meaning. Also, there is an ability to read independently with genuine understanding simple books and items and to write and spell with accuracy ideas appropriate to their age. This level is reached by some first-graders, many more in second grade, and those with personal difficulties or problems in third grade. Occasionally, we meet the whiz who is already on this level in kindergarten.

The *Third Functional Level* occurs when the readers' skills of word recognition and comprehension make them independent of help in word recognition, use of dictionaries, indexes, and reference materials in the classroom and library. In both writing and speaking, they reveal their growing intellectual maturity. This level of reading is reached by the one or two most agile at age six or seven, the majority at the age of eight to ten, and the less verbal one or two years later.

One can readily see how much more descriptive it is to refer to a youngster according to reading level than to grade level. Once this terminology gains wider use, the problems created by the grade level misnomer, the pressures and the problems of failing should be eliminated. Also, the respect for individual differences can be honestly expressed by recognizing each child's level of reading development rather than referring to some as *below grade, up-to-grade,* or *above grade.*

One more key point: because the three levels are predicated upon a broadly based reading program, the tendency to limit reading activities to the narrow competency techniques so widely advocated should be lessened. Instead of teachers and parents pressuring children to do well on tests, the program will expose all to a process of reading to use, to enjoy, and to add to their many learning experiences.

First Functional Level in Reading

Competent educators who have been concerned over the grade classification of youngsters have tried a number of experiments. The one that seemed to satisfy their search for a better way to meet individual differences was by grouping three ages together: five, six, and seven; six, seven, and eight; and others. In such grouping, children who were less mature could work with the younger, the more agile with the older. Emphasis was on the nature of their work, not their age or so-called grade placement. One teacher described how some could be working with those who were already beginning readers, but were less agile in art and rhythms. She recognized the variations within each child.

A common practice is to retain slower five-year-olds in the kindergarten two years. Unfortunately, the term "failure" may be applied to the children detained—a label that still persists, though it is rejected by sensible persons.

There are some wise and sensitive educators, up to date and concerned about the total well-being of all children, who wish that the teaching of individuals and small groups of the one-room rural school would become today's organization, but with no reference to grade level. This idea need concern no one; it's too far off.

It is possible, as is being demonstrated in good schools, to meet the variety of backgrounds and abilities *and* keep the focus on broad reading goals within our present grade organization. Those on the first functional level in reading are the ones just getting acquainted with letters, recognizing their names, making first stabs at writing a letter or two from the alphabet, and occasionally recognizing at sight some popular word such as "Zippy," the name of the classroom's pet bunny. Some in first grade and second grade are also on this level. They are normal youngsters, but slower in verbal matters.

Some at six are where others in the group may have been at four or five. The reasons for their present status may perhaps be the result of illness, some traumatic experience, overprotection, neglect, or a naturally slower pace. A few may fairly tear ahead, once relieved of hampering causes; others may plod along.

All need to feel welcome, in the right place, and glad to be there. No one can produce this effect except the teacher. A major part of such a result is caused by demonstrating to the child very often that he or she is learning, getting along well. To a child a day is a long time, so positive recognition is needed often. Would that it could be at least once a day! Encouragement to a child for a specific step taken adds to the willingness to do more, to go on. Individual praise is often needed, especially by the slower children. They need more proof of their adequacy than those who can dash ahead, although all, including adults, need an occasional "good" or "well done" boost.

Many experiences suggested for those in kindergarten can be helpful for some sixes. But with this age, the program must include opportunities with guidance for the continued progress of those who already have acquired some word recognition techniques, a larger vocabulary, and a wider acquaintance with books. These signs indicate that the youngsters are entering the *Second Reading Level,* that they are progressing in managing some reading by themselves, independently. This point—*their independence*—is the major goal a teacher should work for with each member of the class.

On a trip to the library, many of them, unaided, can select books appropriate for their browsing or reading. One or two may already be eager to use index files. They are able to aid the teacher in the use of cassettes, in locating materials, and running a tape recorder. Their actual growth from their entrance to kindergarten to the beginning of this new year is amazing, assuming the program is planned to encourage them to function on their own.

TOTAL GROUP ACTIVITIES

Any age group that will spend a year together needs to build a kind of family unity, based on common experiences and personal interactions. Many reading experiences become an important part in the development of this kind of group life.

The way in which a teacher starts the day may set the tone of the day. One group of primary teachers started the day in their classrooms with a daily addition to a chart labelled, "Important Things We Can Do," such items as:

> Belle can ride a two-wheeler.
> Andrew can spell American.
> Jimmy can read every name in the class.
> Bob and Andrea can read the weather.
> Holly can count to 100.

The list of in-school and out-of-school accomplishments grew and grew. Each teacher mimeographed copies of each week's list. And youngsters vied with one another to read the entire list. The less verbal were helped by the teacher or a friend to contribute. It was not uncommon to see two or three children standing before the chart in spare moments and reading together orally.

Also, each child was given a notebook, clearly alphabetized. As soon as a child knew a name or word, he or she wrote it under the proper letter. The teachers claimed this day-after-day experience resulted in a live interest in checking on their own and their pals' growth and in sprouting new accomplishments. "And," said one teacher, "best of all, it takes so little time to follow and check on the work of each one."

Individual and group stories, also mimeographed, were read and enjoyed by the whole group. These also formed a personal incentive for reading. Again, the vocabulary was indigenous to the youngsters who did the narrating. One group at the story hour often requested a child's story rather than a published story. Loud applause was given the child-author or authors. All stories were collected and made into booklets, with children planning the title and cover decoration.

Reading in these classrooms had a local flavor and real zip. A few workbooks were available and some phonic and word recognition games, but their use lacked the social enthusiasm of the creative-experience work.

Perhaps the biggest satisfaction came to those who taped their own stories. The tape was then played for guests, parents, and older brothers and sisters. Youngsters, of course, took delight in managing the playing.

Children love to sing, a group experience that too often gets crowded out of the daily schedule. One veteran teacher decried their music program which "demoted all music to our special music teacher." She began each day with a cheery song, and ended the day the same way. When the song was a new one, she wrote the words clearly on a chart, where it stayed until the children remembered them. "And," she reported "that's how many of these youngsters actually learned to read!" No wonder the community protested when her retirement was announced!

Group unity can be developed in a variety of ways, if a teacher respects its value. The spirit of helpfulness between pupils, the constructive behavior while on their own in group work, the eagerness to come to school—all are expressions of the added strength these youngsters of widely different backgrounds can acquire through planned whole-group experiences.

SMALL GROUP AND INDIVIDUAL WORK

For all, regular group work based on their level of reading maturity is needed. This formerly was entirely determined by a three-level basal reading program. In too many schools, this still continues. But, in a school where neither teachers nor children are denied creative growth, plans that emerge as the work progresses from day to day shape the reading program.

Group 1 may have a word-study program based on a movie shown the day before. Key names and words are written clearly (manuscript writing), children pronouncing or singing out the spelling—M-a-r-y and G-i-l-b-e-r-t—with comments by the teacher, "Point to the tall letters," "Who can find the y?" and other helps.

Group 2 may be reading a story multigraphed clearly, dictated by one of the group and recorded by the teacher. They may enjoy chanting the story together after hearing it read, then reading it to themselves. This oral type of repetition is an essential but too little used form of learning, as pointed out previously.

Group 3 may be ready for more help in meeting long words with common prefixes and suffixes. They may be adding to a list being compiled on the chalkboard.

In a visit to a first grade recently, not only did I see such a variety in the daily scheduled reading hour, but I also saw individuals working alone on some appropriate project, one finishing the recording for the cartoon balloon in a comic mural, another matching a list of common words. Some such group and individual experiences extend over days, others may be one-shot affairs.

GUIDING THE USE OF BOOKS

After a few days in the first grade during which some of the foregoing practices have been in use, a teacher plans a daily period with the pupils who can read from books. If a number of books are available, and none is designated as the basal book, the easiest and most appealing ones should be selected. Three or four copies of several different preprimers, if used, will aid in satisfying differences in pupils' interests and also will encourage comparisons and interchange of reading experiences. This procedure also aids the teacher in getting away from the prescribed one-book-per-class or basic book method that prevents sufficient flexibility to meet the reading needs of the variety of pupils. Pupils are told to look at the different books available and to select one. If the one selected does not seem as appropriate as another, the teacher may suggest that the pupil look at the other book and perhaps make a change.

These books will provide some book experiences, such as reading the title, looking at the table of contents, the lining, and the pictures, and then with the teacher's help, reading one or two stories, but not necessarily the entire book. Reading a book from beginning to end often grows too difficult or too monotonous or too lengthy a task for a pupil having his first book-reading experience. Some, however, not only want to read the entire book, but also reread it, and read it orally to anyone at school or home who listens.

After each pupil in this group, which should include not more than four to six pupils, has been helped to select a story, the children may call attention to words, phrases, or sentences that they can read. Or, the teacher may read the story while the children follow in their books. Then they try to read as much as they can of the first part of the story, with individual help by the teacher. This first reading may be oral or half-audible, whichever seems the natural way for the pupils. Pupils may want to ''practice'' before reading a part to the teacher.

Marked differences in ability to remember words and in resourcefulness in seeking aid may be noted in these first book-reading experiences. After one story is known, and the pleasure of reading it is still evident, another story is begun. To urge pupils to read a story until every word is mastered discourages readers, and also applies a standard that even adults do not achieve in their reading. These stories may not necessarily be linked with any of the ongoing experiences of the group, but their vocabulary and ideas must be within the understanding of the pupils.

It may be found that some pupils who were thought capable are not ready for books at this time. Careful plans must be made for such pupils so that their first reading experiences with books will not prejudice them against future reading. At first they may be invited to be in another group to look at a book, and the teacher may read a story especially to this group. One teacher gave a folder to each child with his name written on the cover. Simple stories were mimeographed and placed in the folders. These folders were their booklets and they learned to read them. This attention satisfied them until they could profit from more extensive reading experiences. A criticism often made is that the vocabulary is not basic—or scientific. Right, the vocabulary is *intrinsic,* intrinsic to the children's background of experiences.

COMPREHENSION—PERSONAL OBSERVATION

In the first efforts of reading, pronouncing the words demands most youngsters' full attention. This is where a teacher is needed. After a sentence or so has been read orally, a short talk about its meaning will insert some attention to comprehension. This is a vital need. Frequently, pupils in fourth and fifth grades are discovered low in comprehension, but glib word pronouncers. Similar effects are also the result of a too prescribed phonic system.

Simple games and exercises are useful, too, in helping a child increase power in word recognition and comprehension. One inventive teacher helped youngsters create games which he duplicated. One game was "What Is My Name?" A simple description, "I have black hair and am tall. What is my name?" was not only popular but stimulated writing and spelling as well as comprehension.

The true-false, yes-no type of responses should be avoided. Even at this early age of six, the error in logic of either-or thinking can begin.

PHONICS FOR THE FIRST LEVEL OF READING

The roster of names when properly used for all the needs of personal identification may make necessary some unusual help in phonics. For example: Clarice and Clarence had to look beyond the clue that was the first to catch their eyes to identify their names. So did Fred and Frank. Lucille and Ellen laughed when the teacher pointed out that both had *twin l*'s, "which we call double *l*'s."

There may be recognition of consonants and vowels. One teacher played a guessing game: "I am thinking of a girl whose name has an *a* sound." Mary was helped by her friend, so she jumped up. The class applauded. "I'm thinking of someone whose name begins with *b*." Baxter popped up at once. Again, applause. This teacher had a knack of stirring enthusiasm and action into all phonics. She also introduced children very early to the concept of nonphonic words by calling them *silly* words; others were *sensible*.

This group developed rapidly in the recognition of families of words, prefixes, suffixes, and some syllabification. Not all, of course, were on a par, but many acquired a degree of word recognition approaching independence with their personally selected library books.

RECORDS OF VOCABULARY GROWTH

For the alert learners, keeping a complete record of their new vocabulary additions is an impossibility. Brief memos of the next steps they need in becoming increasingly independent in word recognition techniques are needed, however. Some schools have record forms for all teachers. Others expect teachers to improvise their own system. The simpler and briefer, the surer their regular use. One teacher kept 3-by-5-inch cards, one for each child. Such notations as "George— Sept. 28—missed *often, glad*"; and "Lina—Oct. 9—Read first story alone" gave the teacher the key points for the help needed and evidences of learning.

The individual dictionary, as previously described, used by many teachers, has been found to be full of educational advantages. Each child meets challenges on his or her level. The child learns to copy accurately, a boost to spelling, writing—and phonics. He or she acquires a respect for the technique of alphabetizing, and has proof that he or she is learning, getting ahead.

One important caution: there needs to be frequent enough repetition to help children remember the words they meet in the reading and even the words they record. Oral review games that they and the teacher improvise add to the learning "for keeps." Teachers who are mindful of the need for frequent chances for the children to read their chart additions and their individual and group stories obviate one of the two common criticisms lodged against such informal practices, namely that children *seem to be learning* but fail to remember later on.

INTEGRATED LANGUAGE-ARTS EXPERIENCES

A teacher, when asked, "Do you integrate children's experiences in phonics, spelling, writing, and reading?" looked surprised and said "How can you help doing it?" A program, not fragmented by too much commercial hokum and supportive of functional reading, makes the unified approach to the language arts not only possible but sensible.

Previous examples, if examined, will reveal how natural, often child-suggested, and spontaneous reading leads to writing; and of course, writing leads to spelling. When children discover the real fun in creating stories, seeing them in print, and reading them, an entirely new attitude toward reading often is developed. And, once they write something of their own unaided, one can almost see them sprout. Such experiences create the motivation that sparks all, even the less verbal, to learn.

Fun with words in oral spelling, too often not used or even permitted with some six-year-old children, also has multiple learning value. For auditory-minded children, it should be a must. They not only need to see words, feel them as they write, but hear them spelled. I was fortunate to have many delightful oral spelling experiences that began with the name of the river near which I lived—the Mississippi. A group of us loved to chant M*i*ss-*i*ss-*i*pp*i*! Chanting the spelling of words can become a musical and rhythmic event. Once youngsters catch the spirit of it, they make up their own chants. All such simple, folksy experiences are invaluable in guiding today's TV viewers into the development of a creative approach to the language arts.

EVALUATING AND TESTING

In the evaluation of each child's growth on this first level of functional reading, nothing can take the place of adults who are observers. Parents get the children's reaction to their work in school and notice how children perform when they read. Parents can not only assess children's attitude toward reading but also their reaction to school in general.

The teacher, of course, sees each one in myriads of situations and, it is hoped, keeps adequate records as a guide. The use of standardized tests can be an aid to a teacher in pinpointing each child's place on a particular test. Most standardized tests for six-year-old children are not reliable evidences of all-around reading growth because vocabularies vary from child to child and from situation to situation. As an aide to a teacher to keep each child in focus, they can be a help. For such use, they should be given several months before the year ends and scored at once so that the data they offer can be used as soon as possible.

For an adequate evaluation of each child's progress, a broadly based list of factors should be used by those guiding youngsters to be functional readers. The following list, checked periodically by one teacher, assured her of each child's reading development:

1. Gives evidence of growth in oral language
2. Shows interest in what teacher reads to class
3. Looks at books, pictures, notices on bulletin board
4. Brings in books, pictures, etc., from home
5. Refers to stories or facts previously heard or read
6. Attempts to read independently
7. Shows preference for stories or books
8. Reveals specific growth in reading
9. Attempts to spell independently
10. Attempts to write independently
11. Information from standardized tests
12. Home attitudes expressed toward child's reading progress

At the end of the month the teacher studied the record in order to see the progress made and the next steps desirable for the guidance of each pupil. She also discovered the lacks that might be attributed to her failure to observe carefully some pupils, or to her omissions in planning the program.

Some pupils were so mature in certain phases of their growth that this teacher did not think it essential to record every evidence of their maturity. Some, for example, talked so freely and with such ability that no jottings were placed in the column titled "Gives evidence of growth in oral language."

Records for older pupils do not require such detail or frequency of review except for pupils who present unusual difficulties and need an intensive period of guidance.

Evaluation or an inventory of growth should be made frequently enough to keep a teacher constantly informed about each pupil's success in his or her use of reading. In general, an inventory should be made more frequently with young children than with older children chiefly because they are not sufficiently mature to call their specific needs to the attention of a teacher by asking for aid, and also because they may become discouraged more easily and acquire wrong attitudes toward reading. No matter what a school's policy about evaluating and testing is, the role of the teacher in planning the policy is imperative.

CHAPTER 8

Sevens and Eights—Second Reading Level

SEVEN AND EIGHT ARE THE MOST *CRITICAL YEARS* FOR A CHILD IN school. The youngsters who up to now have stepped along in regular reading paces will continue to do so unless hampered or impeded by errors and gaps in the reading program. For example, those who are already able to read textbooks and personally selected library books by themselves not only should be given many chances to do so, but should also be given help on deeper comprehension problems, and the beginnings of note writing to help organize material and to remember. Further skill development to increase their word recognition and word meaning power by independent use of the dictionary and glossary also is essential, even if only a few are ready for such steps. One of the problems this age group meets is boredom, often the result of the so-called second-grade curriculum.

Schools in many states have curriculum guides in science and social studies that must be followed. Fortunately, no matter what the topics, books—hardcover and paperback—are now available for the young readers well on their way in the second reading level.

For the majority of both seven and eight-year-olds, required grade-level books can be used. Children often described as "up-to-grade" do need the teacher's help and guidance in such materials and encouragement in oral reading. Help with word recognition techniques also needs to be scheduled on a regular daily basis.

As at other levels, there should be frequent discussion of interesting words. Flat, meaningless words or words so common as to lack interest form a poor basis for these discussions, even for beginners. Unfortunately, most of the words found on beginner's lists are based chiefly on high frequency use—*one, is, the, went, saw, we, then,* and other similar words. Teachers are aware how difficult it is to arouse interest in a reading program that depends upon a daily vocabulary mastery of words like these. Such words are the "glue" words that stick the content together, and are essential for accurate reading. For a few, it may be necessary to drill on these "glue" words. Some seven- and eight-year-olds are quick to forget but slow to catch on.

Those who still have difficulty in managing even simple material independently are the ones for whom these two years are *critical*. At this age they are growing aware of their progress and how they compare with others. No matter how helpful and how encouraging teachers and parents have been, they may feel inadequate. This may not always be overtly shown, but shown indirectly by the lack of the normal zip for this age. For them, work that is appealing is a must.

In a community where high school seniors served as aides in elementary school classrooms, one girl, eager to become a writer, wrote a story for each of the six very slow plodders she worked with as her assignment. The stories were simple. Each child (there were only boys in her group) was the main character in his story and played a daring heroic deed. The response was exciting. Teachers from nearby classrooms came in to observe the serious way in which each youngster read his story, a few with no help. When a visiting teacher asked, "Why do you all like the stories?" one responded, "They go fast." Another said, "Something happens."

These comments were very revealing. When the teacher asked if they watched TV and how long, she got the common answers—"Yes, whenever we can." At the preschool age, youngsters pick up the tempo and excitement of TV. There's a rapid pace and much happens. Much of what is their first reading fare cannot be compared with the exciting and frequently violent actions on TV. The style of the girl who wrote stories for the slow plodders captured their interest, not only because the stories featured each child in a stellar role, but also because there was speed and action.

Today's schools, desperately eager to meet real individual needs now are actually using community resources, especially parents and teenagers. For years teens-teaching-teens has been successfully used even in large urban areas. With the present growth of programs in career development, the lift that teenagers can bring to children of elementary age should gain recognition. A boon to both!

EXTENDING READING, AND NEED FOR INDIVIDUAL CHECK-UP

Formerly, with the beginning of studies in the content areas, the focus on teaching reading was to read every word and to prove success in reading by repeating the text word for word. I've called this the "spit-back" method. There was little discussion in an informal way. The questioner was the teacher who knew the answer wanted, the pupil was the responder who fished to find that answer. The teacher who followed this routine felt success, if the answer was verbally correct. The pupil too felt success. The tragedy was that both were fooled!

Now with a broader idea of the content areas, and the respect for how much children are eager to learn if motivated and stimulated to "turn it on," as they would say, a wise teacher recognizes the value of discussing and probing deeper into their understanding of what they read. Not all they read requires a careful follow-up. Often a mere reaction to a book or story read is adequate. But reading habits that limit or confuse comprehension can get established quickly at this age, especially with the fastest readers.

Larry, who read more library books than any other class member, was asked, "Do you run into any words you can't figure out?" He answered glibly, "Sure, but I skip those." The teacher spent some time with Larry. She asked him to reread silently a short story of *The Blue Whale*,* which he reported he had just finished reading. After he had read several pages, he was asked to read the sentence "Scientists believe that the ancestors of whales lived on land millions of years ago." The teacher pointed to the sentence as Larry looked, then said, "I skipped that sentence."

An experienced teacher can relate in a simple way how one can discover what goes on in this hidden activity called silent reading. Some habits that are formed quickly may not be serious. In Larry's case, he needed, first of all, to slow down and not try to read so many

*Kazue Mizumura, *The Blue Whale* (New York: T. Y. Crowell, 1971).

books. He also needed to keep pencil and paper handy and to record words new to him. He demonstrated no specific lack in phonics; but he did reveal an attitude toward reading that may have required genuine motivation toward purposeful reading. This would challenge his thinking, his comprehension, and change his casual word skipping.

At this stage of independent reading with those who often are quick in answering and seemingly up-and-up, a regular and personal inventory is essential. Organization for such an inventory may vary from teacher to teacher but, if adequate, will reveal each youngster's personal reading habits and skills.

CURRICULUM AREAS OF STUDY—READING TO FIND OUT

Much research and proper concern has been demonstrated over the years concerning *reading in the content areas*. Meetings on this topic are found on programs year after year—and are well attended. Usually the age of concern is the intermediate grade level. Actually, the real concern should be from the beginning of reading as a youngster learns *to read to find out,* to know! In a good school program each child should have read *content* material, such as "Rules for Our New Playground," "Today's Movie: *The Three Bears*," and "What We Did This Week," all seen in a new school that I recently visited.

How we react to information we need is different from how we react as we read a novel, a biography, or even the latest book on the earth's crust. We mentally must underscore key items; we may reread to be sure, we may check our understanding at the end of our reading. Often, this is the occasion when we write memos related to our reading. Youngsters at age seven and eight need to have experiences that involve this kind of reading. Many are able to understand that, as a rule, reading for information is *more compact* with more important ideas to remember than stories have. Therefore, we need to "slow down," stop after a point to think of what we've read, reread to be correct, then proceed again. True, in later grades children may still meet some texts poorly written, and too congested with facts for them to read successfully. Most texts for these grades have by now been revised and new ones are of a more literate and interesting quality. Even so, the ability to read factual material carefully needs guidance, not always for all, but for the majority. With texts too difficult for some readers, the oral discussion of the teacher with those who have completed the text keeps the interested nonreaders in the know.

THE LIBRARY—RESOURCE CENTER

A visit to a school library can give one a key to the reading program and the curriculum of the school. I shall describe two visits made in two schools less than ten miles apart.

School 1

I visited School 1 on a Tuesday morning at about 9:30. The only person in the library was the librarian, the parent aide had not yet come. Not one child was there—population of the school 980. The librarian explained that each of the 40 classes had a Library Day, except the kindergartens. On regular days, the children came to the library to browse on their own under the librarians' supervision. (The classroom teachers during this time had a coffee break.) Children exchanged books and got help in finding a new book when needed. Silence was expected. The same procedure was followed for the next group that entered. The main function of the library, according to the librarian, was to "supply books for recreational reading." Once in a while, as told to me, children from older grades looked up items in the encyclopedia or atlas. No books were withdrawn for classroom projects.

School 2

School 2, in a poorer economic neighborhood, had an enrollment of just over 1,000. As I entered the library, three girls, about aged seven were coming out, talking excitedly, each holding a book. The librarian was with a group of older youngsters, answering a question. Two groups, one of second graders, one of fifth graders, were at separate tables, taking notes from books, talking quietly and so interested I was not noticed. Later I was told the second graders were the "reference book committee" that got whatever was needed either for their study on health or new science books with pictures, or good storybooks. The

fifth graders were getting ready to make their report on water conserva-
tion. The librarian said as a result of their study, these youngsters
recommended the library get more up-to-date material.

My evaluation, briefly, was that Library 1 needed no professional
librarian—nor any reference material. The use made of these resources
did not warrant the expense. The reading program of the school could
scarcely be called "literate." But most serious, what a waste of human
resources—child power!

Another excellent chance to evaluate the quality of a school's reading program is the public library. Today's public libraries—most on
skimpy budgets—have programs for preschoolers and older ages.
Books, movies, and interesting demonstrations of crafts and all arts are
presented. Also the staff includes a librarian for children. These de-
velopments have come about through parents' interests and truly literate functional reading programs in schools. Children, eager readers, at
an early age learn how to use this added resource.

At this critical age of seven and eight, the libraries, school and
public, can expose youngsters to the excitement of how much there is
to read, how much there is to know, and how exciting it is to be able to
read.

BOOK CLUBS, COMICS, AND MAGAZINES

At this age, peer pressures become noticeable. One child gets a
magazine as a birthday gift, and it becomes class news. The stampede
is on. Or a youngster struts in, wearing the insignia of a book club, and
the sales pitch runs high—at home. Also comic heroes and heroines
begin to appear. All of this is "super" as these youngsters would say.

Those of us fortunate to recall the anticipation of receiving a
magazine issue, from our own subscription, can recall how avidly we
read, cover to cover. And we remember the eagerness with which we
waited to get our town's newspaper to read our favorite comic strip.
Today's youngsters, in spite of TV, react in the same way. But, today,
book clubs of high literary and factual quality are available, and
magazines, for the youngest, as well as preteenagers. This is the reading so wisely sponsored by parents. Later, a chapter is devoted to the
privilege and responsibility of the parents' role in reading.

CRITICAL ASSESSMENT

After these two years of careful guidance of increased independence in reading through growth in word recognition skills, wider and deeper comprehension, and real reference work in gaining information on essential curriculum topics, many are ready to take on most any challenge of the third and mature level of reading.

Children in a narrow inadequate program may meet the expected results on standardized tests in sentence and paragraph comprehension and other skill measures. But what evidence is there that they are acquiring the habit of reading to enjoy, to discover, to find out? Only a wider basis for individual assessment, which includes the careful notations of the teacher about each child's thinking applied to ongoing curriculum studies in relevant books, personal reading, and the independent use of the library (as described in Library 2) can furnish these data.

What about those three or four youngsters who need help in unravelling words and may even get stopped by the simple words others learned a year or two before as sight words? If the main five goals of teaching reading have been kept in the forefront, these children, too, enjoy reading, use it up to their degree of independence, and demonstrate good work habits in using materials and experiences that help them. And especially, they also enjoy school and get frequent proof of their learning.

CHAPTER 9

Tens, Elevens, Twelves— Approaching Greater Independence

IN MOST CLASSROOMS FOR TEN-, ELEVEN-, AND TWELVE-YEAR-OLDS, the range on all facets of reading varies widely. If all have had the personal help needed and have remained challenged by reading experiences then all, no matter what level, should be eager to continue at their pace.

In this time of mobility, teachers now meet more transferred pupils, some from narrow, unliterate reading programs. At this age, fellow pupils are often more helpful in acquainting classmates with "how it goes here" than the teacher. From their own experience in looking after those who missed school, they can be called experienced tutors. The practice of developing teams of those who tutor and those who need tutoring adds to a wholesome climate like that of a family.

In the initial acquaintance period, a teacher facing the need to keep all challenged finds out not only the reading power of each, but what magazines, subscriptions, book club memberships, and press and comic interests are represented in the group. It is also helpful to know which ones already have membership in the public library, their movie and TV use, and what common interests—such as baseball and gourmet cooking—adults and children share in reading.

No teacher should be shocked to find some still needing help on the simplest reading materials. Word study skills of the first and second reading level may be a must for them. Others, more independent, will be able to deal with some ideas in a text, able to listen and learn and enter into discussion, yet not be able to read without considerable help.

DEVELOPING PATTERNS OF READING BEHAVIOR

From the age of ten, eleven, and twelve, strong trends in attitudes toward learning, self-discipline, and interests become apparent. Peer influence often is stronger than either home or school influence. This period of development demands the most challenging curriculum—and the most challenging teachers. It is also the time when those who have problems, reading and others, should be given the best special help home, school, and community can afford.

Many by this age have acquired good study habits and are personally responsible for homework and continuing projects and promptness in time schedules. It is hoped such pupils are in the majority. Those less mature in habits and still dependent for daily guidance in all reading experiences should spend time with a reading specialist and a school counselor. If, after careful analysis, they are found to be working up to their ability, pressure to improve will have an adverse effect. These are the youngsters for whom a program in the junior high school and later years should be centered around nonacademic work. To date, this is the group most frequently denied appropriate education, especially in communities with too few pupils for a diversified program.

Even so, where conscientious efforts of home and school work in tandem, the results have been very gratifying for all, especially the student. The common phrase "He has found himself through this course" tells a stirring story. With continuing emphasis on career education, more educationally appropriate programs will be developed.

USING CHALLENGING EXPERIENCES AS THE
BASIS FOR INTEREST IN READING

A teacher needs a frequent reminder that an emphasis in the curriculum on experiences that are particularly challenging to the children, experiences that they are eager to talk about, work on, and remain interested in, is the first prerequisite in guiding pupil growth in independent reading. Such experiences make a pupil ready and eager to become a critical reader.

If there is one outstanding obstruction that the teacher meets in attempting to guide pupils in developing a critical type of comprehension, it is the curriculum in which the major emphasis is placed on getting pupils to remember daily lessons from uniform textbooks—day after day, and page after page—lessons unrelated to the needs of the particular pupil, his or her interests, the time of the year, the location of the school, or any other circumstance of importance. In such a curriculum the pupil cannot read and test ideas in terms of their use for his or her purposes. Problems may be set by the assignment, and a marking system may serve as an incentive to read well; but such challenges to the pupil lack the personal or group interest necessary for the development of deep, pervasive, and critical comprehension.

In meeting an array of interesting topics, the child acquires a vocabulary of meaningful, dramatic, and vivid words. These words in turn may form the basis of word studies that lead to the development of important techniques of word recognition.

In recent visits to a public school in which teachers are developing a curriculum based on rich, challenging experiences, I noted various activities that provide challenging experiences. Preparations were being made in the second grade for a trip to see where commuting pupils lived. This was a part of the study of "Our Town." Eleven of the thirty-two pupils were brought to school daily by bus from nearby localities which the majority of the pupils had not seen. On the board was a large map drawn by the teacher showing the routes to be traveled and the names of the towns to be visited. Children wrote their names on the map near the name of the locality from which they came. Each pupil had a mimeographed list of "What We Want to See," which had been compiled by them on preceding days as preparation for the trip.

Pupils in the fourth grade had made a pet census of the school. It had previously been decided to write a book on care of pets that would be sold to pet owners. The list they compiled, however, included not only cats, dogs, and birds, but also a salamander, goats, sheep, rabbits, pigeons, turtles, gerbils, snakes, ants, and white mice. The children were revising their previous plan because their list became too long but they had not yet arrived at a satisfactory decision, although a new study of "What Help Our Library and Homes Offer on Each of These Pets" was indicated as one of the next things to be done.

These activities were not the only ones going on in these groups at that particular time. They are cited here to show the interesting quality possible—indeed essential—to stimulate a pupil to see the need for and resulting value in reading. Compare the ways in which two pupils read a magazine description of the first locomotive. One pupil reads the account as a lesson and is able to recite precisely every detail included in it. Another pupil plans to paint a mural in which the locomotive is to be depicted; he or she reads the description and evaluates it in terms of his or her purpose. There may be several items mentioned in the article that are not visible in the picture included in the text, some descriptions may be too vague to be used as a guide, and necessary detail may be lacking. True, not all reading need be of this exacting nature, but there are times when this critical, careful kind of reading is necessary. When pupils are frequently guided to read to meet important, personally challenging needs, this type of careful reading occurs, and consequently they learn to adjust their method of comprehension to fit their purposes in reading.

It is important to note, though, that the pupils engaging in the experiences briefly described needed additional work to gain knowledge and increased growth in reading from these experiences. If pupils are to glean from a curriculum based on experiences all the relevant, essential learnings possible in each experience, a teacher must be sensitive to the inherent possibilities. Opportunities are then afforded the pupils actually to deal with them. Unless the teacher makes a planned, careful survey of the learning possibilities for the different pupils in each experience, they may skim over lightly and emerge little wiser except for a glib speaking acquaintance with the subject. A check also must be made on the extent and quality of a pupil's reference reading. Reviews and summaries of previous related-learnings also are essential.

DISCUSSING SPECIFIC WORDS FREQUENTLY

Frequent use should be made of stimulating discussions about various words encountered that are interesting because of their meaning, sound, configuration, or uniqueness. It need not be a scheduled part of the daily program, but it must be frequent enough to help pupils to acquire an ever-increasing independence in the techniques of word recognition. In general, it is best to study a word as soon as its importance to the meaning of an experience is noticed.

Pupils may be ready to deal with meanings of interesting words and use them often enough in an exploratory way to annex them to their growing oral vocabularies. Interest in the sound or meaning of words should not be regarded as a welcome by-product of experience; it should be developed by the teacher because it is an *essential* part of a rounded language growth. It also forms the basis for further growth both in oral language and in reading. Again, the words should be interesting to the children and not simply dull vocabulary drill words.

CONDUCTING PLANNED DISCUSSION

The use of vivid, searching discussion about topics and stories read is essential to the development of reading comprehension in all grades, and can be made a part of every kind of school program. Absence of discussion even in a program based upon significant experiences may result in careless, inadequate reading comprehension. In order to have any real effect upon thinking essential to comprehension, discussion must be planned and studied so as to throw light on the specific questions that follow:

1. Are pupils growing in the ability to discuss what they read with a vocabulary sufficiently unlike that used in the reading content to show a general understanding of the ideas? Which pupils verbalize, give back the words they read?

2. Are pupils growing in the ability "to think with, around, and beyond these ideas"? Which pupils can be glib but miss the key points for which they read? For example, in a discussion in a sixth grade about an article describing the completion of the first transcontinental railroad, one pupil gave a summary of the event in his own language, seemingly indicating that he understood the ideas well. When asked, "Was the route any help to New Englanders who wished to go to Florida?" he replied, "Yes, because they could go from north to south without stopping."

3. Are pupils referring to previously learned facts that are related to the topic of discussion? The ability to see the connections or relationships between relevant facts is an essential quality in good reading. The teacher should observe which pupils remember facts read previously and bring their previously accepted ideas to bear upon new ideas. Where this ability is not developed in reading, a pupil may not be able to distinguish between conflicting facts, errors, and intentional deception.

A fifth-grade pupil who was reporting on the climate of Florida as never cold but "always warm, most of the time hot" was not disturbed when he read the newspaper headlines, "Killing Frost Hits Florida Fruit Trees." When asked by the teacher, "Is this what you would expect of Florida weather?" He replied, "Yes, it often freezes the fruit trees in Florida." The teacher then reminded him of his previous statement. He had difficulty seeing the contradiction.

4. Are pupils growing in the ability to appraise the adequacy or completeness of information contained in descriptive material? A fourth-grade boy who was reading a story of flying remarked, "I'll bet the author of this story has never been up in an airplane." When asked why he thought so, he replied, "The story tells so little about planes." Yet many readers, even adults, do not sense the lack of completeness after reading only a cursory article on a topic. Satisfaction with meager information inevitably leads to lack of thoroughness in the pursuit of important problems and also prevents careful evaluation of content. At ten and older, children are able to sense the difference between knowing a little or a lot about a topic.

5. Are pupils learning to evaluate reading material in terms of its intended use? A story may be interesting and entertaining, but its author may not have intended any part of it to be taken for fact. Pupils must learn to recognize the purpose of the author. In a study made by the writer, pupils of fourth, fifth, and sixth grades were found willing to apply ideas gained from fairy tales, imaginative paragraphs, and other obviously nonfactual material to problems in science, history, geography, and health. Guidance in comprehension must help each pupil to appraise content in the light of the author's intentions. Some stories are true-to-life and include facts that are authentic; some are not based on facts. Stories must, therefore, be discussed in terms of such questions as, "Could this be true? What proof can you find for your answer?" "Did the author write this to tell a story or to give information?"

6. Are pupils becoming increasingly aware of authors, their fitness for writing, and the relation between who the author is and how authentic and dependable is the information? For example, in discussing the desirability of a hawk as a pet, a fourth-grade group that had just read *This Hawk Belongs to Me** raised questions. Who was this author?

---

*Jo Polseno, *This Hawk Belongs to Me* (New York: David McKay, 1976).

Was this an absolutely true story? And, did the author really know a lot about hawks? They decided to ask the fifth-grade teacher, who knew the author, about him. Such inquiries may not occur often, but they must be frequent enough for the pupils to learn when they are necessary and also how to proceed.

Another phase of the study of authenticity, especially important with older pupils, leads to development of the ability to recognize propaganda or exaggerated or dishonest advertisements. Since the use of newspapers not only is encouraged but is absolutely necessary to a good, vital curriculum, guidance in the use of all parts of a newspaper becomes necessary. Young newspaper readers, even some in the primary grades, can be guided to understand the difference between fact, opinion, and intentional misrepresentation.

Discussions that reveal answers to such questions as these are essential in teaching pupils how to acquire some of the broad interpretations and understandings of what they read. Two important suggestions should be made, however: first, such discussions must have real life and interest-holding qualities; and second, they must be considered *learning* experiences by pupils and teacher. And, remember one caution: a situation in which a good discussion is interrupted by the teacher saying, "Now let's stop talking and get to work" is discredited in the minds of the pupils and is obviously not recognized by the teacher as an experience in which valuable learning is taking place.

FACING SOME PROBLEMS

The road to such intelligent guidance of maturing readers may not always be smoothly paved. One factor that causes teachers difficulty in developing real understanding of ideas in reading is the lack of appropriate materials. Unfortunately, in the lives of many children, there still is a serious shortage of suitable material for reading. Their homes may be without one newspaper, comic strip, magazine, or child's book. I've only recently been in a home where there were three TV sets, but no dictionary nor encyclopedia. (The mother formerly taught high school math and still substitutes.) The public library may be meagerly stocked with children's books or may be too remote; and the schoolroom may be oversupplied with many sets of books that one-half to two-thirds of the class are unable to read. Some teachers try to meet this problem by attempting to help their pupils recognize and pronounce correctly the obstructing words found in this too difficult material. Such attempts have little effect upon subsequent comprehension and obviously do little to stimulate a greater desire to read.

LACK OF TEACHER EDUCATION IN TECHNIQUES

Another handicap often faced by teachers is the lack of previously acquired techniques for guiding pupils in any but a mechanical recall kind of reading. All too often a narrow process that demanded "reading to give back" was emphasized in their own education. Many of the materials of workbooks reinforce this emphasis. The teaching of reading that enables pupils to acquire a growing ability to deal with the full meanings of what they read demands that teachers themselves not only appreciate this way of reading, but also know how to guide pupils to acquire it. And let it be repeated that this guidance needs to be a concern of all teachers, those of beginning readers, too.

ESSENTIAL: A TEACHER WHO IS A CRITICAL READER

Foremost among the prerequisites basic to teaching today's child to become a critical reader is a thinking teacher who regards the development of thinking readers as the most essential goal in the teaching of reading. One teacher pursuing this major goal alone may run into obstacles; yet there are such valiant teachers. The teacher who functions in a school system where the entire staff aids and abets this major goal is fortunate. Luckily, there are many such schools.

Let us look more closely at the teacher and the teacher's role in reading. A teacher who is a critical reader and who is independent and honest in his or her reactions can be aware of reading situations arising in or out of school that call for guidance in children's understanding. A teacher who is not an astute, experienced reader can scarcely be regarded as being capable of helping children to become so. It should be stated quickly that this is not the fault of teacher education per se; it is, rather, the omission of focus on this need in all education, including the kind of education offered in many liberal arts colleges. Many adults who have become alert critical readers have become so through their own powers. Some may have resorted to helpful books and pamphlets available on how to increase one's powers in thinking and improving comprehension.

In-service programs for educators have helped lift the sights of teachers in careful evaluation of methods to improve teaching. Many schools have incorporated excellent methods into the total program as a result of the study of teaching science. The "scientific" approach to studies has added greatly to an emphasis on abilities demanded in real comprehension.

READINESS FOR JUNIOR HIGH SCHOOL

If it seems that undue attention has been given to the multiple skills demanded in comprehension, one need only to recall my major concern about reading: to acquire for enjoyment and use the ideas enclosed in print; or why teach reading? At ten, eleven, and twelve years, the preteen age, youngsters are ready to become almost fully independent in their own resourcefulness. Once they enter junior high school, the assumption that they have such independence may present them with work beyond them but no aid like that supplied by intermediate grade teachers. Not only that, the realization of their incompetence at this age can be devastating. Therefore, all effort must be exerted to meet each child during this third-level period with properly gauged personal guidance.

Today's schools are making strident efforts to ease the adjustment of new entrants to the junior high school. One significant step is the result of teacher readiness, readiness to be able to help youngsters make the adjustment, especially in the demands for independence in reading, reference work, and good organization and expression in writing.

The biggest aid, however, is the kind of education these youngsters have experienced as ten-, eleven-, and twelve-year-olds. Those who have acquired facility in working on larger projects than the formal day-to-day assignments find the adjustment relatively easy. They are ready for the education tasks now required. Those less fortunate in their elementary school background may not fare so well.

Standardized tests at the conclusion of sixth grade indicate the reading level on a grade level basis. But this is only a part of the reading growth. The tests do not indicate the lack among those spoon-fed youngsters who can meet only short answer and daily assignment jobs. They have been denied the more mature level via personal and curriculum pursuits possible in the third level of reading.

CHAPTER 10

More Suggestions for Developing Critical Comprehension

TODAY'S AVAILABLE EXCITING NEWS EVENTS ON NATIONAL AND local levels offer real competition to the curriculum. One fourth-grader, who transferred from a live, alert school to one in which he said, "All we get are dead lessons," asked, "How does anyone keep up to date in this school?"

Challenges are acquired from three sources. The first should be an essential part of the school's curriculum. With the rich possibilities in the various sciences, and the continuing unravelling of new discoveries on planet earth, all that's needed is a teacher who wants to keep up to date, as any adult citizen should, and the school leadership that not only permits teachers to keep up to date, but encourages them to do so.

In one school, which I visited to increase my faith in education, I met with the intermediate grade teachers. I had just visited the various groups to hear reports on "What We Are Following Up." One boy, aged eleven, from the least affluent family, had saved his money for a trip to Mystic, Connecticut. "When I first went there all I wanted to see was a live whale. Now, I'm interested in whales and all marine life." Another said, "I'm interested in excavations. I want to see where they have dug up dinosaur tracks." The class librarian, a very slight girl of only ten said, "I can't keep up with all the new books we are getting for science reading."

The eagerness to report, the enthusiasm, and the evidence of careful reading made me ask the teachers, "How do you develop this?" One, who called herself "The Matriarch," said, "All you have to do is to have a ten-minute period the first thing in the morning and ask, "Who has something new and interesting to report, that's all." Again, this is what a live program from kindergarten on can develop.

The second source of challenge should come from the local or state sequential plans especially in the areas of health, science, and social studies. A text written years before cannot include a current springboard for the topics, but an alert teacher and youngsters can. Relevance keeps education "respectable and up to date" in the eyes of youngsters, even as young as eight.

In my classroom visits, I frequently ask "Have you been studying something that I may not know about, and maybe your parents don't either?" In classes where good discussion is a common practice, I get some fascinating responses. Only recently, one child said, "Do you know about the new plate theory of the earth's crust?" The teacher said, "His father is a scientist so he keeps us ahead of the pack." Many topics not so far out were referred to, such as "Did you learn about insecticides when you were in our grade?" and "We go to the Museum of Natural History once a year. Did you ever go to a big museum like that?"

The third source of challenge can readily be seen from these brief accounts—personal interests and hobbies. One sixth-grader not only followed the world series but made a scrapbook for class members of newspaper accounts and brief write-ups of sportscasters' reports to be included. "We made our teacher into a baseball fan," gleefully announced one boy. One of the girls said, "You *had* to be a baseball fan around here—and even in some homes."

FUNCTIONING INDEPENDENCE

From their accounts it is easy to see the use and kind of voluntary and independent reading that goes on in that school. School librarians are able to detail the pressures and demands avid readers create—especially with nonelastic budgets. Even children who are seriously plodding along as they read can enjoy books of intriguing topics now simply written and colorfully illustrated. The authors, illustrators, and editors deserve salaams for publishing such books.

In all three age levels, the development of readers ready to read widely and deeply on a topic is not only possible but essential. Today's youngsters, with increased sophistication especially from TV and family travels, are capable of understanding the difference between "knowing a little about dinosaurs" and "knowing a lot" about them.

Opportunities for personal and group reading in order to feel the satisfaction in getting truly informed stir greater eagerness to become truly informed and to gain information on more topics. When a teacher says, "I can't keep up with all they read," one knows his or her group is really busy reading; the contagion of such interest affects all. If some remain uninterested and unmoved, they reveal the need of personal intensive study. In a good school, such personal help usually occurs before this age. There are situations, however, when a youngster, once full of reading eagerness, pulls back. The cause may not be easy to locate. The need for understanding and corrective help is immediate.

COMPREHENSION AIDED BY DISCUSSION

We are often startled by the kinds of comments and questions ten-year-old children insert. At times we say, "They are sharp thinkers." At other times we regret that they are not sharper. This is the period in their school careers when learning to think straight is imperative—yet all too often absolutely neglected. The pressure on *basics* in the minds of too many still means return to memorization, not necessarily with understanding and appreciation. In a classroom where hour after hour is used for silent exercises from texts and workbooks, the chances are high that full use of thinking potential is not being developed. Although questions and exercises in up-to-date texts now demand provocative thinking, the full possibilities in such materials are not developed silently. Oral discussion in a classroom climate where the teacher encourages honest and divergent responses is so important that more attention should be given to it.

COMPREHENSION—PROBING WITH REASONS

For decades, the major focus in teaching comprehension has been: "What does it say?" The child who could give back a satisfactory answer was considered a comprehending reader. Gradually, teachers became aware that a child who answered by repeating the words of the book might not understand but might merely be parroting words. The child was then asked to "tell in *your own words.*" Many youngsters were thus brought closer to dealing with the meaning of what they had read, obviously an essential step in comprehension. The technique did not go far enough in terms of a child's growth as a thinking—at times even a reflective—reader.

The teaching that transforms the child into a comprehending reader must include training in the ability to probe, because most of this age group are intellectually ready for it. It should also include more of the preparation necessary to keep our oncoming young citizens from perpetuating some of the glaring errors so often made in our adult society. Both elements, their readiness and society's need, must be used as guidelines in the reading program of these intermediate-grade years. If these young people are guided to become thinking readers, our land will more surely maintain its lofty ideals of freedom.

A characteristic of this group, as revealed by research, is that they are becoming influenced by some of the symbols and conditions in our life. They are beginning to classify people as rich or not so rich, as influential or inconsequential, as in the right group or not in it. Materials are judged as up to date or fossilized, as approved by friends or not approved. Youngsters at this time seem to be testing out the ability to make up their own minds, being independent as with the newfound power of riding a two-wheeler or going to the shopping area unaccompanied. They give signs of stretching their thinking, too, in more adult ways. This, then, is an important time for the school to make a conscious effort in guiding their thinking so that they make worthy choices instead of the common errors described in the following section.

Error 1. The Short-Answer Habit

Extremely common among the unfortunate errors found among adults is the *short-answer mentality,* as it has been dubbed. We know that many of the problems we meet cannot be solved in one-word answers—yes-or-no, right-or-wrong, do-or-don't. Yet many adults are impatient. They want a quick answer, as in the case of the parent who, during a conference about her son, said to a fifth-grade teacher, "Tell me in one word what's the matter with him. Is he dumb, or lazy, or what?'' (The child, incidentally, was an overweight boy with little athletic skill, whose twin sister was a star in all school sports.)

We might appropriately ask if the schools' extensive use of short-answer, true-false, yes-no tests and exercises has added to this impatience. We know that the anxieties of this age have also developed much of it. Once teachers become aware of this practice of short-circuiting essential thinking, they may limit their own use of the techniques that encourage it and take more time to teach the qualities inherent in good thinking. Such questions as, ''Can we answer this quickly or is this the kind of question that should take more time and more careful thinking?'' and, ''Should we examine this point more carefully?'' if frequently asked, will help children acquire a more thoughtful approach to serious matters. We can so teach them that their important decisions are less likely to be fraught with danger. One can imagine the results to the child if the teacher in the incident just mentioned were addicted to short-circuited thinking. If so, she might have said ''Well, he's lazy,'' and the mother might have ''seen to it'' that the child put more energy into his work. Unfortunately, we see all around us unwise decisions made upon the basis of such short-answer thinking.

Error 2. The Quackish Generalization

Equally erroneous and even more frequent are generalizations made without adequate data. Our reading materials are filled with them. Some time ago, two widely read books critical of today's teaching of reading were studied for this error in thinking, and each example was underlined with red pencil. The books are a startling exhibition of red-lined pages. Such statements as ''None of the children in our schools,'' and ''All of the teachers in the schools'' occur again and again. Imagine an author being so insensitive in his or her thinking as to overlook such a common error as making sweeping generalizations with insufficient facts.

One alert teacher started to correct this error in thinking when a boy, a newcomer to the school, came in to her first-grade classroom during morning recess crying. The teacher asked sympathetically, ''What's the matter?'' He said, ''All the kids hit me.'' She said, ''All the kids?'' ''All the boys,'' he answered. ''All the boys?'' ''Four or five.'' When the children reentered the room, she asked this youngster to point out the offenders. He looked around carefully, then said, pointing, "That one." The teacher then said, "This *one* boy hit you," and proceeded to ease the situation.

Actually this six-year-old was no more erroneous in his sweeping statement of "All the kids" than are some of our so-called educated adults. Children in a fourth grade under excellent teacher guidance discussed a newspaper editorial in which the editor urged the police force to get busy and squelch "this North End behavior." Two boys from a section of town called the North End had thrown stones at passing cars. Some of the fourth-graders lived in the North End. They felt the sting of labeling the misdemeanor of two boys by the generalized term "North End behavior." The teacher commented that after the discussion of this condition, the children tended to check one another on their own statements and demonstrated genuine concern for greater accuracy in relating incidents.

Bias and all forms of prejudice flourish under this same brand of crooked thinking. Of course, once alerted as were the children in the fourth grade just described, a beginning is made in preventing this error. "You can't trust these foreigners," "Girls are no good in science," and "Teachers make poor parents" are flagrant examples of such erroneous thinking. The teacher who hears a child state a generalization of this variety and says, "Let's pause and examine this," is not only doing an essential job as a teacher of good thinking and of more adequate reading comprehension but also as a builder of a better citizen.

Error 3. I Don't Know, but My Mind Is Made Up

Another evident quirk in thinking is the premature closing of minds to additional essential facts. We commonly regard people who make a practice of reacting in this way as opinionated. One of my sharp encounters with this kind of reaction occurred years ago in Minnesota when voters were to decide upon the state's right to enter the field of paving highways. Heretofore this right had belonged to the city or the county. I chanced to meet an acquaintance, a one-time high school valedictorian, who, I thought, would be enlightened on this issue. "Tell me your views on the coming vote on the referendum," I asked. "I assume you've gone into the matter." Without a moment's pause he said, "No, I haven't gone into it, but my mind is made up. I'm voting against it."

Incidents of this kind are met by fourth-, fifth-, and sixth-graders. These youngsters are ready to become aware of the errors of thinking inherent in such situations and are ready to be educated so that they will not follow in similar patterns. Here one must stop to ask: was any effort made in the education of adult delinquent thinkers to direct them along proper, sensible ways of deciding what to believe?

Error 4. Specializing in Snap Judgments

Not too unlike the "know-it-all" is the thinker who makes weighty decisions in the ticking off of seconds. There are many occasions when snap judgments are demanded, and often one only has time for these. The truly wise person, however, if circumstances make it possible, takes the time needed to study, read, ponder, and finally, to make a worthy judgment. Knowing when we should suspend a decision is in itself a major step in learning. Again, evidences of teaching this concept as policy can be found in fine educational environments.

Pausing to think may seem to run counter to our swift-paced age. Yet the seriousness of the decisions required of us should argue that for our own safety we must make deliberation in decision-making a routine practice. The place to acquire this practice in the course of our normal living is in the elementary school, especially in the intermediate grades.

THREE BASIC STEPS IN GAINING READING COMPREHENSION

Reading comprehension can be analyzed in many ways. It seems relevant here, in light of the foregoing descriptions of common problems in clear thinking, to examine reading comprehension in terms of thinking abilities the reader is asked to use in common kinds of reading.

Step 1. Understanding Items and Their Relationships

Understanding items and their relationships is essential in carrying on every kind of reading. The reader must be able not only to recognize the meaning of items within a story or article but also to understand the relationships among these items—from the beginning to the end of the reading. This process is the first step in achieving comprehension. A child's ability to carry out this procedure is examined by a teacher in asking a pupil to tell what he has read. For example, in an account of why water, when it freezes, breaks a covered glass, the pupils of course, need to recognize such words as *covered, freeze,* and *expand,* but then they need to understand the causal relationships among the items.

Step 2. Reacting to What Is Read

Reacting to what is read, naturally, is a highly personal process. A child may respond to reading by liking, not liking, accepting, or rejecting, by being challenged to think further or by being indifferent and giving the content no further thought. His reaction will depend partly upon the kind of child he is. Much reading is not remembered because it is not considered important.

Both children and adults often use these two steps in reading stories and accounts of incidents. Following the reading, they could pass a test on the items included; they have understood in a cursory way the ideas the author conveyed, but they are not sufficiently interested to give the ideas further thought.

Step 3. Probing Deeper

We probe deeper into reading that we assess as important. Teaching in this area of the reading process may suffer because of lack of classroom time or inadequate regard for its importance, or because the teacher is unsure of her ability to pursue it.

This step requires many abilities. These vary with the individual's purposes in reading, the nature of the material, and the reader. In some readings, a person must be concerned with the competence of the author: Who is the author? What is his or her background? What qualifies him or her to write on the subject? A group of fourth-graders, reading a book about the South Pole in which polar bears were mentioned, raised such questions. They had studied explorations of the South Pole and had read that there were no polar bears at the South Pole.

At other times, implications, shades of meaning, and emotionally colored words must be recognized for what they are. The fourth-graders who resented the implication about North End behavior were applying this ability to their reading. In each case, a child must have the ability to get at the meanings inherent in the lines per se; then he or she must seek beyond the lines for deeper meanings in order to comprehend them fully.

DEVELOPING INDIVIDUAL REACTIONS

Through basic comprehension and the selective powers of children their taste is encouraged. A teacher interested in probing taste, preferences, or individual reactions periodically takes time to discuss stories and articles that several of the group have read. To have value for both teacher and pupils, this discussion must be guided in such a way that individual youngsters not only feel free to react but wish to do so and will do so honestly. The teacher's expression of respect for each child's view and the teacher's manner of sharing it will evoke such honesty.

One wonders, harking back to the frequent criticism of adults in the United States who reveal sheeplike tendencies not only in styles of clothes and homes but also in their reading, how much effort was invested in making yesterday's children—today's adults—independent in preferences. One might also question whether there was an ample supply of widely varied materials to challenge all tastes, and whether there were many occasions for browsing, sampling, and discussing. A reading diet of identical texts scarcely stimulates individual reactions.

A classroom in which the teacher asks for opinions and gets them in unison is not a wholesome place in which to develop independent thinkers. This is a typical "yes" atmosphere in which individuality, integrity, and thinking are soft-pedaled.

AND LASTLY, TIME AND COURAGE TO THINK

Time is an important factor in developing reading comprehension. To ask, "What do you think about this news item?" of a group of alert children who are developing the power to react demands that the teacher allot time to listen to three or four pupils, and some comments that may be unfolded slowly. A fifth-grade girl, in commenting on what was wrong with her school, said, "I don't get time to think. Nobody does. We are all too busy."

In addition to having time to think, each individual needs the courage to do so. As one examines the way in which a comprehending reader is educated to bring his or her personal feelings and attitudes into the process of appraising and selecting and to voice these feelings, one sees immediately the relationship of this stage of reading growth to the increase of the child's integrity and moral strength.

It is not easy, even in an excellent classroom situation, to state a divergent assessment of reading matter. For example, one girl gave her view of a popular natural science series that was appearing in the local daily paper. "I don't like these science stories," she declared. She then gave her reasons: animals talked; essential data were omitted. The articles were "dressed-up science fiction." Not all her fellow students were in agreement. A teacher, aware of the strong pro and con attitudes that even very young children develop, must be ready to help youngsters in such situations to respect the speaker's forthrightness and courage. Those who do not agree with the viewpoint may be encouraged to analyze their reasons for differing and to state them.

It is a privileged classroom, indeed, be it a kindergarten or an upper grade, in which "This I like" or "This I don't like" are honored statements. In the "everybody does" program in which 100 percent agreement is sought on most matters, children are being denied the chance to develop taste, the chance to learn how to read before arriving at convictions and outlooks, and the chance to become honest, wholesome, strong personalities. They are being denied an opportunity to test themselves in standing up for what they believe; instead, they are being encouraged to ape our Caspar Milquetoasts of standard design.

CHAPTER 11

Guiding the Progress of Slow Learners in Reading

MUCH OF WHAT HAS BEEN WRITTEN IN THE PREVIOUS CHAPTERS pertains to slow-learning readers as well as to successful readers. The difficulties met by teachers in aiding some pupils in reading growth, however, are so persistent that particular attention should be devoted to this important responsibility.

Readers who are designated as slow or "below grade" can be classified in three groups. In the first group are those pupils with some real block to reading development. This block may be due to visual, auditory, or oral handicap, or to some emotional or neurological disorder. Some pupils present a problem of diagnosis and guidance that usually can be met only by specialists in ophthalmology, neurology, or clinical psychology. They require technical remedial guidance in reading in order to become successful readers. A teacher may, with expert advice, aid them in the remedial work and promote their development. Sometimes, the best the teacher can do is to create a cooperative class atmosphere to which they can contribute to the extent of their ability.

In the second group are those who are retarded readers. Their full reading development has been arrested for some reason, such as delayed entrance to first grade, irregular attendance, transfer from another school, unfamiliarity with the English language, or negative home environment. With appropriate individual guidance, sometimes for only a short time, they strike their normal stride.

In the third group, and this is the largest of the three groups, are those pupils who are slow in developing such skills as reading and who will continue to be slow in their progress.

This chapter will deal with some of the essential ways of guiding all in their reading development.

The assumption that persists that all pupils in a grade, with the right kind of help, would achieve a grade standard in reading as well as in all other areas is erroneous. Even if they are properly taught and if they put forth sufficient effort, some, especially the third group, may not become fluent readers. The selection of uniform books, the use of uniform methods, and the expectancy of uniform learnings in the curriculum is grossly inappropriate for these pupils. One of the most undesirable results of these practices is the effect upon the pupil, who, sensing that he or she is "inferior," "below grade," or "subnormal," loses interest and even acquires great distaste for everything related to school. This attitude will slow up any progress, and often encourages defensive behavior and ultimate truancy. Much also has been written about the loss of sparkle to the bright, who too have been cheated and retarded by this quest for the grade norm—the sacred cow.

EARLY DEMAND FOR SPECIALISTS' AID

Fortunately, through a variety of health, education, welfare, and religious organizations, physical examinations of children bring to parents' attention such defects as visual and auditory shortages, and emotional difficulties that become apparent in preschool years. More careful attention to all health needs in kindergartens is also prevalent. In spite of home, community, and school efforts, some youngsters get to third grade and even later before some real physical and emotional block to learning is analyzed. The correction for each child demands school and home cooperation to secure the appropriate specialists' aid.

Teachers often receive suggestions from specialists as to their participation in a given case. Where these instructions are understandable and workable (in a classroom of twenty-five or more pupils), teachers have become not only cooperative but more informed. Large, urban-area schools do include a multidisciplinary staff; smaller local schools rely on local or nearby specialists. The first group of so-called retarded get their help through such cooperative efforts. Actually, they should not be classified as reading problems.

SPECIAL HELP CASES

In the second group are a number of children considered below-graders; many with warm personal attention suddenly make up for a lack of progress. This so often is the case of school transfers. Moving from one school to another, which often means moving from one town to another, may be a traumatic experience, especially for the younger school members. With normal intelligence, and a supportive home base, such below-grade children latch on quickly and need no further help.

Those with irregular attendance, too, can take hold and "catch up" if their attendance becomes regular. In our large urban areas, wise school policy is to invest in teacher-home-and-counselor matters involving attendance early in the child's school life—before the truancy problem has developed.

In all of this group, known to be of normal intelligence, according to teacher and test information, encouraging individual help and aid within peer groups usually puts these children back in normal learning behavior. Today's informed teachers, with a variety of commercial materials and their own inventiveness, actually make possible ultimate success for these youngsters, not only in education—but also in constructive behavior.

THE ROLE OF THE READING SPECIALIST

Much will be left unwritten in this capsule description of the work of a key person in our schools, the reading specialist. The rapid increase in numbers of those with special work in the reading program is evidence of both the need for their expertise and the value of their work. Their function, when properly used, helps children and adds to teachers' know-how.

Many of the children previously described do not actually need the help commonly called *remedial* work. As previously described, sensible efforts by the classroom teacher, peers, and family bring these lower achievers back into bloom. To assign all such youngsters to a reading teacher or specialist lessens teachers' growth and effectiveness. For example, in one school, the common practice was to send any child who had been absent three or more days to the "remedial room.'' Teachers in that situation, according to my observation, paid little attention to individual differences. One, in November, still did not know the background of two very noticeably disturbed boys. This situation, it is to be hoped, is not common. Formerly, some schools assigned all children with problems to the reading teacher for a once-a-week remedial treatment. Of course, children forgot the help and directions they got from week to week. Due to the heavy load of this teacher, nothing was accomplished.

There are a few conditions, which, if applied, make the reading specialist, or special reading teacher (one with expertise in reading) an invaluable member of an elementary school staff:

1. The person selected should be able to get a quick, accepting response from the children. Often, more than the expertise, the manner in which a person relates to a youngster in need is the key to success. The same kind of warmth is needed in relation to the teachers with whom a congenial cooperative relationship is a must.

2. The person selected needs not only a knowledge of good teaching practices in addition to remedial techniques, but also considerable depth in child psychology. The latter is essential because the reading specialist should be one of the team who helps in diagnosing those who need the care of a specialist beyond the school's realm.

3. Children who are found to need help in reading beyond the teacher's ability should be aided in whatever adjustments are needed when the daily special reading help creates an interruption. This includes making the program so acceptable to all classmates that no child is stigmatized. The closer the work of the regular classroom and the remedial work can be kept, the better. This, of course, requires good teacher-specialist communication.

The sudden surge of this area of specialization in our schools has already proven its value, especially when careful knowledge of the primary group reveals the beginnings of difficulty.

ENGLISH—A SECOND LANGUAGE

Real progress has been made in the teaching of English to the non-English-speaking youngsters. As early as 1933, Junius Meriam's two-year study used the language experience approach to teaching

Mexican-American children with great success.* A study of how a child acquires his "mother tongue" sheds light on how a child acquires English as a second language. I presented key points in chapter 1, "Language—the First Step." Through early experiences, a child latches onto words, phrases, idioms, pronunciation, and stress. The best examples of how children acquire a second language, I've observed, have been out of school, on school grounds, in parks, at cub scout meetings, and children's parties. Where children are active and socially free, they pick up the language they are experiencing. We have reading experts at work on this language-experience approach, as Maryanne Hall has so clearly presented in her work.** With their help and the classroom teacher's wise aid, this will no longer be considered a problem. We in the United States for too long have acted as if we were a linguistically incompetent nation, while children from Europe enter our schools and speak two and three languages. The need for debunking our once-a-week special lesson plan, or the use of a ten-minute tape recording exercise is long past due; it seems we are now moving in a promising direction.

GOOD BUT SLOW IN PERFORMANCE

Children of the third group, as I previously referred to them, are perfectly normal in every way, but they react later than others, need more help in remembering and in becoming independent, and seem less alert in general. To dub them remedial or special—or anything else—can be gravely injurious. For too long, society has not only subtly but overtly mistreated them. Even parents show a preference for the quicker and a rejection of the slower. For some, special classwork has given them a chance to develop to full capacity and to become, later on, economically independent. For others, regular classroom work plus special help or some form of "mainstreaming" has been successful. For many, individual help at their level in a regular classroom has been just right. Suggestions, all taken from clever teachers

---

*Junius L. Meriam, "An Activity Curriculum in a School of Mexican Children," *Journal of Experimental Education* (1933): 304–308.

**Maryanne Hall, *The Language Experience Approach for Teaching Reading: A Research Perspective*, 2d ed. (Newark, Del.: International Reading Association, 1978).

who faced the needs of the slower with real imagination and professional zeal fellow:

1. Get to know the child to see what interests and appeals to him or her. Establish contacts in conversation with the child around these points, even if only in small snatches of time. This will help to get him or her to be open-faced and friendly with you.

2. Get acquainted with his or her reading growth to discover: (a) the child's attitude toward his or her own effectiveness, (b) what the child enjoys about reading, (c) what the child likes least, and (d) what he or she is ready to start with—on trial. Good diagnostic work in reading utilizes the child's own interpretations of his or her reading status.

3. Invite him or her to share in planning the next steps. The child's reading work can be a partnership arrangement. If the child doesn't try—or if the teacher doesn't—this venture, like a business partnership, may become a flop.

4. Encourage the child to start on a small unit of work, a short exercise or a brief story, as a trial balloon. If this goes well, he or she can plan a bigger job next time. If it can be related to the child's interests, all the better. The main point is to encourage the child to want to try his or her reading skills on it. Be at hand to help and encourage.

5. Encourage him or her to share in the evaluation. A slow learner needs to grow in saying, "This is OK," "I'm not sure here," and, "I know I didn't get this." Self-appraisal is often needed by these youngsters who have lost confidence in themselves and settle back to accept whatever anyone tells them of their work.

6. Help the child to keep some record of his or her successes. Learning to read heretofore may have been a big, vague, hopeless task for the child. He or she needs to see the milestones of progress.

When I worked with Floyd, an eight-year-old in third grade, who said he hated even to try to read, we started with the names of things he liked—*wirehaired fox terrier, xylophone, jigsaw puzzle,* and *Edgar* (his pal). I wrote these four items in my best manuscript writing on separate 5-by-8-inch cards. Then I suggested, "See how long it takes you to know what is on each card. Get anyone to help you and to try you out." By noon Floyd said, "I know each one, test me." He did and, bursting with pride, said, "I knew what *xylophone* was but Edgar (who was an able reader) didn't." What success he chanced upon!

Then we developed a system: he would tell me which words he wished to have written on cards, work on them, and, joyfully, would watch his card pile grow. As I wrote, we'd spell out and pronounce the words. In three weeks Floyd was reading books as well as second-grade readers.

Floyd, like most slow learners, needed the feedback from seeing his progress accumulate. Some concrete evidence, such as a stack of cards or a pile of completed exercises, helps highlight *big* steps. Progress that is scarcely noticeable discourages slow learners as it does able readers—even adults. We like to see that we are getting something accomplished.

7. Give the children opportunities to report progress to their class members. So often slow youngsters have had little opportunity to swell their chests and with uninhibited pride report on a success.

A wonderful teacher in her late sixties had the fourth-graders who were in a slow group in her room make individual progress reports whenever the children thought they were ready. The entire class then gave them rousing applause. The effect was not only effort-boosting to the slow children but also gave a sense of helpful sharing to the more facile youngsters. This teacher had great success each year with heterogeneous groups, their range of ability often from grade 1 to beyond grade 6. What a teacher!

8. Arrange for teamwork. Two or more of equal or unequal ability can work together reading a book or a story in a reader or doing a page from a workbook or skill test. If the children who are teamed up enjoy one another, learning is enhanced. They often are wise choosers of work companions. If their relationships create a too strong reliance of one upon the other, a time for changing teams is indicated.

Team reports of "what we did together" are boosters for additional successful efforts. If the arrangement is between a successful reader and one less apt, suggestions on how to help and how to give the partner a chance may foster increased value. Such efforts also prevent a class from becoming divided into haves and have-nots over reading status.

9. Help a child acquire the language with which he or she can report success. Often slower readers are not facile in their language. In response to a question raised at home, "What are you doing in reading?" one may say, "Oh, I'm just working." In talking with this child after he or she has finished a piece of work, help the child in a specific

way to see what was accomplished. For example, "You remembered, Donald, these three hard words today, *that, start,* and *now.* Now you tell me what you did that was good." Help him to repeat your comment. It may be a real satisfaction for him to mention his success to a few of his class neighbors. Introduce the idea by some comment as "Listen, Donald has a report to make of some success he's just had."

10. Use stories on records or tape for which books are also available. Teach the child how to manipulate the machine, how to use individual earphones, and how to follow in the book as he or she hears the story read. Some children have reported that this was their most helpful reading experience.

11. Plan to have a daily help period. A special help period once a week, whether with a classroom teacher or a specialist, seems a questionable policy. Children, even self-propelled learners, forget from week to week. I found teachers, competent adults, in weekly evening classes claiming they had to develop special techniques of note-taking and reviewing in order to feel any continuity from week to week. Careful observations of children in various time schedules favor the daily plan. Even on a daily plan, some may need help in remembering "what we did yesterday."

HOW MUCH CAN BE ACHIEVED?

Will all slow learners with good teaching assistance blossom forth? Would that there were a never-fail formula or a real panacea to answer that question. There are children difficult to handle and seemingly blocked in ability to understand, to remember, or even to be attentive. These are the ones often called real "problems," who need the individual attention of a psychologist, a guidance person, or a reading specialist with a good background in mental hygiene. They may be bright children who up to the present have not taken hold for some hard-to-detect reason. Or they may be children already too frustrated to try once more.

Various efforts in behalf of serious reading disability cases are observable in good schools of today. One impressive fact is that blame is not lodged against the child. Instead, the attitude expressed is, "We'll try to find a way to help you." In ceaseless efforts, ways often are found—usually highly personal—tailored to fit the needs of the particular child.

To prevent problems from getting deep, schools now give more detailed attention to slower achievers in the primary grades. Help is offered by classroom teachers, and outside the classroom by specialists, to be sure everything is done to get these young plodders to become more self-reliant before they enter junior high schools.

Looking back over several decades, one must be impressed with the progress the schools, valiant teachers, administrators, and specialists have accomplished in recognizing individual differences and in developing school programs that are actually guiding youngsters to be self-propelled, critical, and functional readers.

PART 3

Reading for the Future

CHAPTER 12

Parent Power

NO ARGUMENT IS NECESSARY TO CONVINCE ANYONE THAT LEGIONS OF parents today, and over the years, have been responsible for the success of children's reading. Long before the term *parenting* came into usage, superb parenting was being practiced. Living and learning together in previous years was a condition of the times. Much work demanded parent and child as a team, transportation made fewer inroads into family unity, and movie, radio, and TV had not yet replaced family games, visiting, and creative pastimes.

Yet, there remains a vestige of the fear created by so-called scientific educators who advocated a hands-off policy for parents, lest they do the wrong thing, ruin a child's vision, or misteach him or her. At a parent group discussion recently a mother expressed this fear.

One relaxed mother of four immediately rose and gave a brief account of how her four youngsters learned to read before entering kindergarten.

Bob and I took turns holding Ed on our laps and reading to him— whichever book he brought us to read. He'd turn the pages, once in a while ask, "Where does it say that? Read that again," and once in a while, "You skipped a part!" We knew he followed closely so were not surprised when he read more and more by himself. Now Fred was different. He's always been an artist. We had to write captions for his pictures. Then he wrote them on his pictures—not with a crayon—with a pencil. Gradually he was reading. I should really call my kitchen my reading laboratory, because that's where Beth learned. She'd say, "Tell me what to get," when I was baking. She could get salt, cinnamon, ginger, anything. And she would look and look at the recipe whenever I used one. Now, with young Mable, Beth is teaching her. They play school by the hour and Mable is going into kindergarten like the others, a reader.

This mother would be shocked to learn of the millions of government dollars (from our taxes) that not too long ago had been spent in efforts to find the *one best way* to teach all children to read. Some few kindergarten teachers show displeasure over prekindergarten readers: "They spoil things for us," meaning the children don't fit certain regimented plans. But such teachers are a diminishing breed.

PARENT INFLUENCE BEYOND EARLY YEARS

The continuing interest in children's big business, which is their education, also pays high dividends. Some of the ideas in this book that I've gleaned from parents reveal the enduring influence of reading in the family, not only on the child's learning but on bond-building family ties. Only recently, while at our local library, a boy about twelve approached the librarian and said, "My dad's sick again. Do you have any new science mystery, the kind I like? Dad always reads the ones I bring home." How much this incident told of father-and-son relationship.

ABOUT THE NONACHIEVERS

Always being reasonable in what we expect of children may entail a hardship for us adults. If normal, happy, pigtailed Judy doesn't master the complicated translation of clusters of letters to their correct words during the month, we feel our whole family tree is tottering in a destructive wind. We often feel that we must explain Judy's difficulty to friends and neighbors; we joke about "the beautiful but dumb member of the family"; we may even pretend that we are glad to have a "problem" child. All this is rather certain evidence of the deep humiliation and disappointment we feel because Judy—rollicking, fun-loving Judy—is not such a success in reading.

All of us who observe children—teachers, principals, and parents—should know that learning to read with ability, to recognize and remember more and more words, begins with some children even before kindergarten age, with others at six and one-half, seven, and even later. A careful study made years ago in the then Lincoln School, of Teacher's College, Columbia University, disclosed that children whose beginning in reading was postponed until after the first grade, caught up with, and in many cases even excelled, others who had started earlier. Some children mature more slowly than others. But, why worry? Look at us relaxed adults, who dare scan the formulas pertaining to atomic energy, but who cannot begin to tell what they mean. We feel quite adequate in handling our duties in daily life, however. Let's give children the same right to be themselves!

ONE WAY TO HELP: TAKE TIME TO LISTEN

Even on the busiest days, take time to listen to children while they relate incidents. Wait for the child to finish his or her sentence, and then ask reasonable questions that will elicit an elaboration. For example, when young John rushes to the kitchen to tell his mother, "The announcer on TV said a blizzard is coming," a quick display of interest and a further question, "Did he say when?" or "Are you sure he meant here in our section?" not only will establish a fine bond of give-and-take between mother and youngster, but also will indicate to the child that mother is interested in his or her reporting. Consequently, the child is inclined to remain alert, and eager to share. In addition to developing good family and group relationships, such moments are very important. If we want to assure reading growth and interest in events, being attentive as the child tells and retells happenings, and being challenged by them, makes for good habits of listening, recalling, and comprehending.

For Millie, a younger reader who in the middle of breakfast may remark, quite unrelated to anything that has been said, "I can tell a capital Q from an O," such an answer as, "That's fine," is inadequate. The child wants to relate a discovery. Give her a chance; ask how. Perhaps she will even demonstrate by getting a pencil and paper, yes, to the extent of interrupting her meal. This is a red-hot moment in learning. Take time for it.

Similarly, when a child calls attention to a picture or an article in a magazine or book, stop, look, and listen. This is reading at work. Therefore, recognize it as such, even if it costs a momentary interruption. Or, if an interruption at that time is too costly, say, "Wait a moment," and then, as quickly as possible, take time out to listen.

Readiness to listen, if continued, can prevent the generation gap some parents now assume *natural*. Sharing interests about books and articles and news events can make for easy conversation and comfortable questioning and sharing of divergent opinions. This process develops naturally if started when children are young.

One father, who had to travel too much to keep a close contact with two boys, one eight and one ten, said he studied how to get close to them conversationally and hit upon an idea, "You be my secretaries. Save any headlines from the sport page or any other part of the paper that you think I'd want to know when I get back." Their efforts grew and grew, so did their common reading interests and the bond between father and sons.

Be reciprocal; share choice items with youngsters. A father said to his young son, "Here's something in the newspaper today about Jack's father that will interest you," and then read to him, "Mr. O.H. Daniel has been named the new scoutmaster."

Many such incidents cannot be planned in advance, but they are too important to pass unnoticed. They help lay the groundwork for talking things over, exploring ideas together, and giving and accepting advice. They help create a wholesome atmosphere for learning.

FIND OUT TOGETHER

Another enjoyable way to encourage reading is to find out things together. Children, if encouraged and treated understandingly, will bombard adults with questions. At two, these questions, "Why, mommy?" "Why, daddy?" may not mean more than, "Here I am. Talk to me." But let's be aware of the moments when a child's questions are real questions. "What makes that noise in the cleaner?"

"Why don't you want any bread today?" and "Where did Aunt Sally go?" may take time and thought to answer, but answers are essential to keep this important asking-to-learn growing. We can often discover how important the answer is if we have an opportunity to listen to the child's subsequent conversation. A little girl of three, when told not to play with the telephone, asked, "Why?" and her mother explained. Later that afternoon, she approached a neighbor and offered this, "When you come to our house you can't use our telephone—it bothers the operator." Children ask questions seriously, and they accept sincere answers with equal seriousness.

Children's questions can get adults into some hot pursuits of information. When Jean, aged nine, asked, "When was the first automobile made?" her father at first replied, "I don't know." Her brother, aged thirteen, said, "I read it once, but I've forgotten." Now the subject could have been dropped at that point, but the father, who truly enjoyed finding answers for such questions, suggested a careful search be made. The hunt, which became a family project, finally led to the encyclopedia. This is an excellent example of an attitude toward the use of reading in living that adds so much to the zest and fun of life. As long as there is enthusiasm in finding out, life has sparkle, and learning takes place for children and adults.

One very stimulating teacher, of sixth grade, reminded children when they met an interesting fact in science or social studies, "This is the kind of fact your mother or father might want to know." The youngsters now are planning a skit for parents' night at the school, "Stump the Experts." They are digging out ideas from their reading to use as questions. It is hoped the parents are "ready."

SHARING CHILDREN'S INTERESTS

Another prerequisite for establishing a suitable atmosphere in the home is nurturing worthwhile interests. Children are always interested in doing things. Often, we adults, tired after our daily duties, are faced with youngsters who are filled with vitality and eager for new fields to conquer.

Going exploring together and sharing in fun and discovery with youngsters of all ages are excellent ways to develop worthy interests and keep within the "interest-range" of children. Those of us who are considered "old fogies" by children may not be old, but somewhere along the line we lost contact with their budding interests, and we seem out of touch with things important, *their* live interests. The result—the generation gap.

PARENT AS CRITIC

It is very important how we accept the children's work that they bring home to show us. Taking time to look and hear it described lifts their effort in importance. Pictures, spelling papers, or any written work that they voluntarily present calls for parent reaction. At times, the item may be a disappointing product to the pupil. He or she may be asking for specific help and encouragement. If one senses that a youngster is not putting forth effort, always wants praise, but is building inner standards for poor work, helpful but firm suggestions are needed. "Is this the best you can do?" when asked in a casual manner—with a pause for an answer—may evoke an honest "No." "O.K. let's see your best" may be all the prodding needed.

Bribing and rewarding may get transitory improvement, but it fails to help the youngster build inner standards and a real desire to want to do good work. A family in which parents and children dare admit not always doing their best creates a climate in which all can be honest. If, however, no parents' efforts get a youngster moving, a conference at school should be sought.

Periodically, parents, too, need to take stock by asking themselves, "Have we been enjoying learning something? Have we shared our satisfactions with the youngsters? Do we read together? Do we take time to discuss some news?"

A boy of twelve began writing a serial titled *The Adventures of Teddy the Terrible*. Each episode was full of slapstick humor and harrowing "death-defying" escapades. At frequent intervals, the whole family was asked to listen to a new serial—hot from the writer's pen. This writer later read his serial in the classroom, where he had a larger audience. Undoubtedly, this experience had real value in sending this boy along to satisfying reading as well as writing pursuits.

READERS ON THE HUNT

Some of these episodes may seem far removed from children's learning. They really are not. A life full of the fun of doing things together and the satisfaction of sharing experience with an interested family is bound to develop many powers. One of these powers is sure to be the continued satisfaction in widespread, voluntary reading.

Let us look at some simple happenings to see how they expand into significant learning. A girl, a little over six years of age, took a walk regularly with her father, and older brother and sister on Sundays. She became sign-conscious. She noticed names on store windows and mailboxes, numbers above doors, and street signs. The other members of her family joined her by chanting in unison, "Fourth Street Bakery," "Dr. Blake," "Ninth Avenue North." Reaching home, she wrote, after a fashion, some of the signs that she recalled. She displayed her efforts to her family; they were pleased, helped her correct her writing, and answered her questions on what she wished to write next. From this free and easy family fun the child began to read, write, and spell.

Older children are able to apply their interests and skills differently. Three neighborhood boys, their ages ranging from ten to eleven, organized a Yankee Fan Club. They read the sports pages of the Sunday paper, and from it clipped pictures and stories about the Yanks. They solicited the help of older sports fans in collecting information about the team; they wrote the manager for pictures and souvenirs to put in their trophy room, located in a club member's garage. The city librarian was approached to see what materials she could offer. So was the school principal. The project received community support from adults who recognized the importance such interest had for the wholesome growth of these boys. Reading magazines, newspapers, and books grew to be more fun for them. Typing, printing, and writing labels became a necessary project. And filing and cataloging eventually had to be learned as their collection of materials grew.

A similar example of learning growth occurred in a rural community. Two youngsters, a brother and sister of about twelve and fourteen years of age, had been drawing, painting, and collecting flags. They became interested in gathering information about flags, their origin, and use. Their study led them to history books and encyclopedias in the school library, and to the historical society of the county. During their summer vacation, they developed a quiz program for a fall school assembly in which appeared such questions as "Where did the flag fly which inspired the writing of the 'Star Spangled Banner'?" "What was the largest number of stripes our flag ever had?" and "What is the Union Jack?"

Such pursuits as ship and airplane building, dollhouse furnishing, stamp collecting, code deciphering, quiz programs, TV newscasts, and experimental cookery, when made into family interests, help promote a truly ideal atmosphere for proper learning. From such interests, children not only acquire personal satisfaction, they also come to realize the value of reading and other essential skills. The amount of knowledge they acquire is not only astonishing to adults, but at times can be embarrassing. Their resourcefulness and imagination in turning up new avenues of help often put their more prosaic elders to shame. They were probably reared in a one-book kind of learning. Not to be overlooked, when parents face their shortages honestly, this can be the cornerstone of genuine family cohesiveness.

CHILDREN AS PARENT TUTORS

Widespread experiments have been conducted with children, often teenagers, tutoring other teenagers. Parents commonly report of older siblings teaching the younger. Not often enough do we hear of children tutoring their parents, yet this has gone on in the families of immigrants over the years. The child who got to a school, public or private, and learned to read, write, spell, and calculate, came home and taught; usually the child taught the father, in order to raise his functional level at work. Today's increased number of citizens from around the world has again increased this practice. The danger that the young tutors will become disrespectful or unmindful of parental authority is prevented by the wholesome, law-abiding life parents establish in the family.

A teacher, close to pupils and their families, may become an added source of aid, by offering suggestions, supplying appropriate materials, and showing a willingness to be called on for help. Both child and parent may sprout faster in acquiring not only reading but all the language arts skills so vital for their livelihood. Not to be overlooked is the satisfaction to the teacher, whose role now actually becomes *community educator*.

CHOICE OF VALUES

Time and money create myriads of choices for everyone, and how we spend each depends upon our values. In the examples given, we can assume that parents who spent time, from moments to longer periods, with youngsters' reading valued this as important. Money, too, figures in this picture.

A fifth-grade teacher in a bimodel community—half well-to-do commuters and half factory workers—made a study of the home reading influence on his twenty-nine pupils. This plan originated after the school approved the soliciting of children to join a certain book club. Of the twenty-nine youngsters, nineteen subscribed. Of the nineteen who did, eleven came from the lower economic area of the town. Of the ten who did not subscribe, seven came from the upper economic level. From the teacher's parent conferences, which were scheduled to occur shortly after the book club event, he gathered added information. His conclusion was: first, economic level does not determine time spent with children, their books, and their reading in particular; and second, economic level does not per se determine book ownership by an individual child.

He cautioned that he did not dare to press too deeply in his interviews, but from his cursory inquiry, he thought some parents felt their efforts were not essential in this "book buying" and "reading tutoring business," that they "helped the community finance a good school library, and teachers were paid to teach the kids how to read and how to use the library."

A shocking report! Yet, it demands further inquiry and education for delinquent parents in our so-called adequate economic class. The efforts parents on meager budgets put forth to boost their children's learning may too often go unheralded. Also, the assumptions we make about home environments require a look deeper than common symbols. The important basic question is: What kind of citizens are we bringing up for our democracy? Those who live for personal transitory gains, or those who invest even at great sacrifice for a generation of honest, searching, and intelligent achievers who will contribute to our nation's ideals? As an optimist, I think, as this teacher's study indicated, that the latter are in the majority.

CHAPTER 13

Summary: Some Simple Suggestions

FOR OVER SIXTY YEARS I HAVE HAD A CLOSE CONTACT WITH children's reading, their beginning, their growth, and later development. I have seen the beginning of the so-called scientific emphasis in the teaching of reading, and the numerous materials, emphases and systems that promised that all youngsters would become successful readers—"up to grade level." For me, it is not a difficult matter to select worthy ideas and materials from the sleazy and the spurious. We've taken some twisted paths, but also some sound ones. Today's youngsters, though not all of them, are learning to read; teachers and parents are active in the process, as are community groups and state and national agencies.

Enormous sums, millions, chiefly from the federal government, are invested in discovering, altering, and amplifying how children of all ages are taught to read. Yet there are periodic waves of laments, "Today's youngsters are not learning to read." "We are giving illiterate high school students diplomas." True, in this period, which we can describe as "hectic history," many youngsters from the early years cruise along never meeting their proper stride in terms of their ability. Even so, there are promising signs; we must build on them, as I've attempted to do.

PROMISING TRENDS

The greatest boon for today's children is the everincreasing knowledge of the preschool years. In the three or four years before a child enters kindergarten, he or she has acquired language adequate for meeting daily life experiences, a vocabulary inherent in these experiences, and an amazing amount of know-how about managing the world close by. This development varies according to the family, neighborhood, and community conditions. Those who are in a communicative, receptive home and immediate environment propel themselves with greater ease than those who are less encouraged. Some preschoolers, from their first days, are more open-eyed and alert than others.

The second promising trend to build on is the recognition of individual differences, the uniqueness of each child born. Although this was always recognized and verbalized, today's homes and schools are now far more valiant in their efforts to guide each child as an individual than they were formerly.

The third important promise, expounded years ago in John Dewey's theory of learning, is at last coming to the forefront: the basis of learning through experiences. An observation of young children investigating a new toy or any new item reveals their approach to learning. I refer to them as inspectors because they first of all pause and stare, then they touch, wiggle, and explore. At the one-year age they also taste. When learning a new word, they try sounding out, then they repeat. Their enjoyment in hearing themselves is apparent. So without any special financial investment, the preschoolers "pick up" their vocabulary, their behavioral responses, and tricks of the culture so amazing to those who take the time to observe.

Among the tricks of the culture are symbols, labels on cans, neon signs, and writing. Many, unaided, by themselves figure out sounds and meanings, start to pronounce words they see, and some are eager to begin to write.

Once a child's school career begins in nursery school or kindergarten, wider social contacts, different routines, and new materials and experiences are met.

NEGLECTED IMPERATIVES

Before proceeding to describe the development of each child's reading progress, much needed attention must be given to three common causes of failure. The first is irregular school attendance. This, for young beginners, can be traumatic. Except for the agile and already self-propelled, it may cause a lack of enthusiasm about learning, a dislike of school, and even a damage to a child's feeling of adequacy. For older youngsters, loss of wholesome interests and a decline in personal promise becomes evident. School attendance is a primary responsibility of the family. But personally interested teachers, guidance personnel, and administrators have encouraged, often literally dragged, youngsters without parent help from their tendency to skip school.

The second need is for more opportunity, especially for those in primary grades, to read orally, spell orally, sing, and hear themselves as they transcribe letters into words. Present-day restlessness in the classroom has made many teachers rely on the cut-and-paste, or write-in quiet work, not necessarily as an aid to the students' learning but to help "keep order." Multisensory learning is essential for most of us, especially the less intellectually agile.

The former emphasis on the value of silent reading and its relation to speed still casts a shadow on today's classrooms. Fortunately, there are many teachers who personally recognize the value of oral chanting of poetry or voice choir, group reading, and group singing.

The third need, as equally neglected as the second, is adequate repetition. Those who notice how a preschooler goes over and over a new skill are aware of the essential need of practice—or drill. This last word, due to its connotations of boredom and waste of time, has been so deleted from classroom use as to be responsible for some youngsters not latching onto reading from the beginning. For many, especially the less verbal, their tempo needs not only to be paced slower, but also needs to include more repetition. This, to be truly helpful, needs the variation and sparkle that a good teacher creates. The child needs to see real steps of progress, which stimulate satisfaction and further effort.

THREE FUNCTIONAL READING LEVELS

The main goal in teaching all to read is the development of an individual's ability to translate symbols to meanings. The end product should be the mature reader who can see through the symbols to the meaning as directly as we look at a scene through a window. Just as we are not aware of the glass, the mature reader is unaware of the symbols. True independence is essential in becoming such a reader; there-fore in all teaching, the youngster must be "turned on," interested and encouraged to propel himself or herself, as far as ability permits. Furthermore, reading will be used to increase the competence in living and its enjoyment. Learning how to read is inane unless it is inherently a part of the use of reading to live.

These last two points—independence and function—are too often submerged, even neglected, by the emphasis on grade level achieve-ment. Actually, the description of a young reader as up to grade level or even beyond grade level gives no information about these main purposes in teaching reading. Instead of using this terminology, a description of how a child grows from a status of young nonreader to a reader able to use dictionary, index, glossary, and reference material while reading material appropriate to his or her interest level, reveals three specific levels of growth that are more descriptive.

First Level of Functional Reading Growth

The first level of growth in functional reading starts as preschoolers notice signs, words on TV, labels. They may also watch closely as a person writes or reads a letter. These first experiences are a powerful learning—they mean that symbols convey meanings. Gradually, specific letters or words catch their attention. Often this happens with no adult or older sibling giving a suggestion. Children who are read to, from even as early as one year, may acquire a fund of details, many considered "reading-readiness" items. They can acquire a wide range of stories, poems, and jingles, know-how to handle books, and a waxing eagerness to demonstrate what they know.

Kindergarten children at the end of the year, when properly ob-served, reveal a wide range; some are just beginning to take a second look at a word or a letter, others already can read simple books.

The Second Reading Level

There is no sharp line of demarcation between any of the levels of reading. Once youngsters begin to apply the simplest items from phonics, have a growing sight vocabulary, and are full of eagerness to read "what they know" independently, they are ready for the kinds of experiences that stretch their vocabularies and require new techniques in unlocking words and in using new resources for help. For them, the so-called reading-readiness programs are not only a bore but actually a hindrance to growth, whether they are in kindergarten or first grade. They are ready for reading, relating and writing experiences that extend their know-how in word recognition techniques and in getting ideas from their independent reading.

This stage, if properly guided at school and at home, is the period in which the greatest strides in word recognition are made. Some, even at six and seven, are ready, perhaps with help, to explore dictionaries, not only as a spelling aid but for meanings. The majority, however, move slowly but surely from kindergarten through first and second grade in regular but less spectacular steps. They may need help, stimulation, encouragement, and much repetition. They can share many of the daily reading events with the rest and glean often more than a teacher expects. They are book selectors, book readers, beginning writers, and storytellers. They too will reveal dogged determination to read a group story or item from a book or to pronounce a new word with independence.

Some, less alert, may reach this second stage at age eight or even later. All, however, need to acquire ways of helping themselves, of remembering, of using techniques, and in following ideas as they read materials appropriate for them.

The Third Reading Level

We all have heard a seven- or eight-year-old say, "I can read almost anything." This may be a sudden realization that occurs to youngsters on the third reading level. For the majority, such reading competence occurs at nine or ten, for some a year or two later. None should be regarded as stellar, none as retarded. Each is pacing growth according to the multiple factors of life—even as we adults meet our daily responsibilities.

This is the point where guidance too often lags, even misses the main purpose of learning to read—the function of reading. Once the effort to recognize words and to follow a sentence, paragraph, and short selection through to its conclusion has become easy, the use of reading as a self-boosting power for independent and group studies in the variety of content areas is essential. Study techniques appropriate to research, some of which may be brief and some lengthy, are needed.

How to outline, how to keep records, how to extend the use of indexes and other library resources—all are not only needed but give each reader the sense of growth and competence. These study techniques also are called on in many problems youngsters meet every day. We often see youngsters who through their newly acquired techniques become "careful" students, and those who need more direction lest they become "careless."

A successful two or three years of guidance in reading at this age develops readers who are truly mature. From here on, they can manage their education responsibilities with the use of texts, tapes, magazines, newspapers, manuals, and other materials with continued success. The use of radio and TV for their value as resources also is desirable.

Children who have a slower pace may, with enough help and encouragement, acquire a growing ability to manage their studies. Those with real blocks, though, who seem unable to get far beyond the first level, should be given special help as soon as their static condition is noticed. This is a responsibility that schools have taken on in recent years with increasing success.

DEVELOPING CRITICAL READERS

From earliest years, some children are quick to notice discrepancies, omissions, and common errors in our speaking and thinking. Unfortunately, guidance in acquiring the ability to think straight is still least stressed not only in classrooms, but also in professional literature. Actually, the need of children for guidance in their thinking is apparent daily. A study of the use of "everybody," "all the kids," and "nobody" would bring this out clearly.

Added to this serious oversight, is the common absorption of child—and teacher—with the essential business of recognizing words, writing letters and spelling correctly, so that in the total language arts process, the emphasis is on skills, rather than on meaning and personal reaction. Again, some unaided probe what they read and write.

The ability of children to mature in thinking remains to be thoroughly assessed, but with the experiences in a good curriculum, and real, honest, and open discussion, genuine ability to think sprouts; of course, the ability to think permeates comprehending while reading and listening, as well as while speaking and writing. In a free society, such as we strive to maintain, such guidance is imperative. Once begun, youngsters startle adults by calling attention to their use of crooked thinking and twisted logic.

INCREASING RECOGNITION OF PARENTS' INFLUENCE

Information about parent influence on young children's total development is not only extant, but the everyday use of it is increasing. Children's language development, vocabulary range, awareness of their world through a wide variety of experiences, love of books, and beginnings in reading—all are enhanced by good, understanding parents.

This fine influence tends to lessen once children enter school and especially in the preteen years when boys and girls begin to express their independence.

By continued interest in their personal endeavors and by including them in true parent-child team projects, an enduring bond can be sustained. Large areas of common concern with real give-and-take discussion increase the knowledge of adults and their youngsters, while still respecting the need for private interests.

Part of the development of functional reading results from a family's exploration of some interest together. Children enjoy seeing their parents as learners with them, often acting as the parents' informants.

Times do occur when the parent assesses the child's efforts, gives direction, and redirects misguided steps. Such parental help becomes more effective if it is only a part of the parent's life with the child.

The two greatest influences in every child's reading are his or her family and school. Where these two forces work harmoniously with children's burgeoning interests and powers, full release of each individual's constructive power is developed.

Bibliography

Allen, Roach V. *Language Experience Activities*. New York: Houghton Mifflin, 1976.

Chase, Stuart. *Guides to Straight Thinking, with Thirteen Common Fallacies*. New York: Harper & Row, 1956.

Cullinan, Bernice E., and Carmichael, Carolyn W., eds. *Literature and Young Children*. Urbana, Ill.: National Council of Teachers of English, 1977.

Fisher, Carol J., and Terry, C. Ann. *Children's Language and the Language Arts*. New York: McGraw-Hill, 1976.

Hall, Maryanne. *The Language Experience Approach for Teaching Reading: A Research Perspective*. 2d ed. Newark, Del.: International Reading Association, 1978.

Hittleman, Daniel R. *Developmental Reading: A Psycholinguistic Perspective*. New York: Rand McNally, 1978.

Kohl, Herbert. *Growing with Your Children*. Boston and Toronto: Little, Brown, 1978.

————. *36 Children*. New York: New American Library, 1968.

Leichter, Hope Jensen, ed. *The Family As Educator*. New York: Teachers College Press, 1975.

Ollila, Lloyd O., ed. *The Kindergarten Child and Reading*. Newark, Del.: International Reading Association, 1971.

Piaget, Jean. *The Language and Thought of the Child*. New York: Harcourt, Brace, 1926.

Stauffer, R.G. *Directing Reading Maturity As a Cognitive Process*. New York: Harper & Row, 1969.

Index